EXPLORING
SPACE

EXPLORING SPACE

HEATHER COUPER

TREASURE PRESS

front cover: *Space shuttle Challenger c/o NASA.*
endpapers *Some of the 27 dishes which make up the Very Large Array radio telescope near Sorocco, New Mexico.*
half title *Kitt Peak National Observatory 4 metre (158 inch) photograph of the Trifid Nebula in Sagittarius.*
title *Skylab*
this page *Radio telescopes at the Mullard Radio Astronomy Observatory, Cambridge, UK.*

First published in Great Britain in 1980 by
Sundial Books Ltd

This edition published in 1984 by
Treasure Press
59 Grosvenor Street
London W1

© 1980 Hennerwood Publications Ltd

ISBN 0 907812 75 9

Printed in Hong Kong

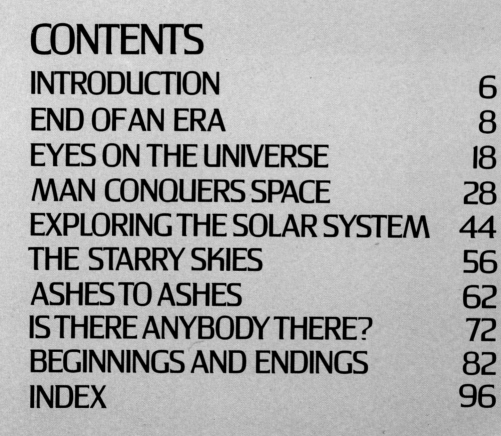

CONTENTS

INTRODUCTION

We stand on the brink of the 21st century — a time long-cherished by science fiction writers as the start of the Space Era. Films, comic strips and books alike have kept alive this vision of effortless space ventures and daring exploits.

Although world crises, budget cuts and political wrangling have conspired to rob space travel of some of its pioneering romance, the wider, long-term view is not so bleak. It is a matter of seeing the Earth and its inhabitants in perspective. While our present troubles may serve to tie us to our planet, we must remember that the Earth is just an insignificant speck circling one of the hundred million million million stars in the Universe.

The riches of space are far greater, socially and economically, than anything we can hope to find by staying at home. And, in the last resort, we are star-children — not mere Earth-dwellers. Everything on this planet, including our own bodies, is made of atoms once processed in long-dead stars.

This book tells of the wider world beyond the Earth, from the humble Moon to the awesome quasars. It reports on our first tentative steps as a spacefaring race, and looks to our directions in the future.

This coming millenium will give every human being the chance to break away from his native planet. What will he find out there?

left *England and Wales, seen from Earth orbit.*
above far left *The Hale 5 metre (200 inch) telescope on Palomar Mountain, California.*
above centre left *The Rosette Nebula in Monoceros.*
above centre right *The launch of Apollo 16.*
above right *Artist's impression of Uranus, after the discovery of its rings in 1977.*

END OF AN ERA

Ask a non-scientist friend what he or she thinks about when he hears the word 'space'. The chances are that his reply will involve references to killer satellites, intergalactic warfare, timewarps and black holes. Yet only 25 years ago, such a reply would have seemed incredible, to say the least. 'Space', in those not-too-distant days, would have conjured up a vision of white-bearded astronomers peering intently through ancient telescopes late into the small hours of the morning — occasionally discovering a new star or comet. In the last quarter-century, however, there has been a new renaissance in astronomy, comparable with that experienced in the days of Copernicus, Kepler and Galileo. We are living through this period, and everyone's changed attitude to space is an accurate barometer of this rebirth.

There is certainly nothing new in Man feeling that his future — and his destiny —

lie among the stars. Whether true or false, the age-old practice of astrology has always stressed the links between us and the heavens, and today, possibly because of our dehumanizing preoccupation with technology, even more people are exploring these connections to find their personal directions. And Man's urge to fly was as much a romantic dream to touch the sky as a practical economic proposition, but until very recently he was bound to his planet and could only 'stand and stare'.

It is sadly ironic that the end of this era was precipitated by World War II, when practical scientific progress was necessarily running at its greatest rate. The tremendous strides made in electronics, computers, communications and missile technology were the ideal preparation that peacetime Man needed to begin his greatest adventure yet — his journey to the stars. On 4 October 1957 Russian space scientists demonstrated, by

above   *The Moon, Man's first target in Space, photographed by the homeward-bound Apollo 17 crew. On the right of this view is part of the Moon's farside, permanently hidden from Earth.*

right   *Astronaut's eye view of planet Earth, captured in this picture taken by the Apollo 10 crew. The Gulf of California can be seen through the thick blanket of cloud which covers much of the planet.*

the launch of Sputnik 1, that Man need not be a prisoner of the Earth forever; and in 1961 the first cosmonaut, Yuri Gagarin, proved it.

The beginning of the 'Space Age' was not, in itself, the end of an era. The end has come about gradually, as more and more people have come to realize that we on Earth are no longer isolated from the Universe but are part of it, and that it is beckoning with uncharted courses demanding to be explored. Astronomers and space scientists now work together in close cooperation to open up the Universe for the voyagers of the future.

Perhaps the competitiveness of the Russian—American race to get a man on the Moon has obscured this cooperation. Increasingly, however, astronomers are using space as their observatory, to view objects hidden by Earth's churning atmosphere and to touch nearby worlds at second hand. In the past two decades remote-controlled spacecraft have probed our Sun's family beyond the mighty planet Jupiter to distant Saturn. Four Russian Lander craft have now photographed Venus's red-hot surface; America's Mariner 10 swooped low over the craters of scorched little Mercury. Arid Mars has had many spaceprobe visitors, but none so inquisitive as the two Viking craft which made a close reconnaissance of the planet in 1976, minutely examining its soil for possible tell-tale signs of life.

We have also, unintentionally, sent out spaceships to the stars. Pioneer 10, which skimmed past Jupiter in 1973, is now heading out of our solar system into space beyond. Should it by chance encounter an extraterrestrial civilization, it bears a plaque telling its readers all about our planet and its inhabitants. The true starships

of the future, however, are at present confined to dreams and drawingboards.

Returning to the nearer future, there is a great deal in store in the space pipeline for the closing years of the twentieth century. The projects may not hit the headlines as they once did, for economic and political factors have put an end to the time when space was an arena for dazzling exploits. But many countries, other than the traditional 'space superpowers' of America and Russia, now have ongoing space programmes — India, Japan and China, to name but a few. Naturally, the superpowers are still in the lead, and the Americans in particular have a number of planetary projects in progress. Their Voyager 1 probe, which sent back such spectacular pictures of the Jupiter and Saturn systems in the early 1980s, has now finished its task; but its partner, Voyager 2, has work ahead. In January 1986, it will fly close to Uranus, and with luck — for its scanning platform was damaged in its encounter with Saturn — it will send back images of that ghostly, ringed world. In August 1989 it will photograph Neptune.

The Sun and Venus are in for more investigation at about the same time. The US plan a 'Venus Radar Mapper', to map the clouded planet from orbit; while the European Space Agency are at an advanced stage with their International Solar Polar Mission, which will fly over the Sun. The spectacular results from the outer Solar System have prompted more investigation of our immediate surroundings; there are discussions on both sides of the Atlantic about sending probes to the asteroids and into Mars orbit. Further afield, there are plans for a Saturn probe — designed to look closely at its nitrogen-

swathed moon, Titan. The US Galileo mission to Jupiter is on for certain in 1990, when a probe from an orbiting spacecraft will make a suicide plunge into the giant planet's churning atmosphere. And when Halley's Comet returns to the inner solar system in 1986, it will find four spaceprobes waiting for it — two Russian Vega probes, the Japanese Planet A, and the European Giotto.

But it's the least spectacular project which typifies our present attitude to space. The reusable Space Shuttle is at last beginning to make space routine. Soon, we will regard it as an environment like any other — a place for commerce, for industry, for research. This is a very different attitude from any which has prevailed over the countless centuries during which Man has watched the stars.

Some 5,000 years ago Man raised great stone structures at Stonehenge, Callanish in the Hebrides and Carnac in Brittany — monuments which are a lasting testimony to the astonishing technical and astronomical skills of their builders. With these great megalithic observatories astronomer-priests were able to measure the length of the year, predict the occurrence of the longest and shortest days, foretell eclipses and recognize many small but long-term cyclic events in the heavens. How this astronomical expertise was accumulated and disseminated remains a mystery, because Western Man at that time did not leave written records.

Astronomical records do not appear until 1500 BC, in the ruins of the Babylonian civilization. From this time on, the lands of the Near East and those around the Mediterranean Sea became the cradle of astronomy — scarcely surprising when we

below left Saturn and its glorious rings, photographed from 3.4 million km (2.1 million miles) by the retreating Voyager 2 space probe. Some of the fine divisions in the rings are clearly visible.

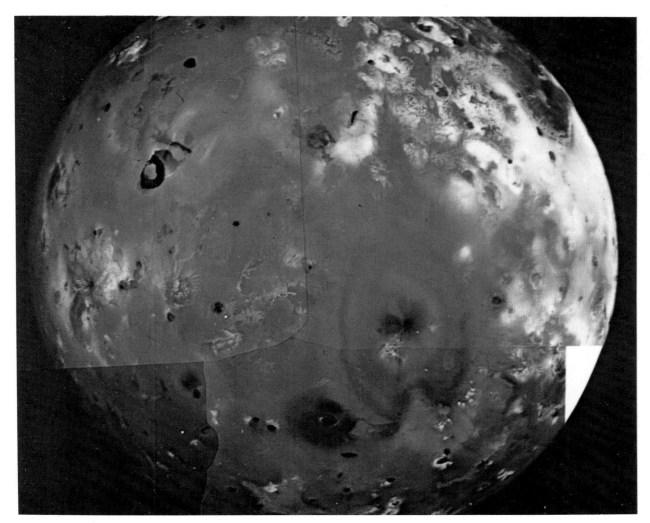

left *Sulphur-swathed Io, Jupiter's most bizarre moon, photographed from 376,950 km (234,225 miles) by the Voyager 1 fly-by probe in March 1979. Before the mission, astronomers had no idea that this small world — the size of our Moon — harbours active volcanoes whose eruptions continually change its surface.*

below *Space Shuttle — extraterrestrial workhorse of the 1980s — poised hundreds of kilometres above Earth's surface. In its cargo bay is the European Space Agency's 'Spacelab' space station, in which teams of scientists can conduct experiments in 'shirtsleeve' conditions (without spacesuits).*

think of their superb weather and abundance of dark clear nights. Although they made maps showing star positions, the Babylonians were particularly interested in the bodies which move across the sky. They believed that the position of the Sun, the Moon or a planet against a particular background of stars had influence on the Babylonian affairs of state, and in those days of political unrest astronomers had an important role to play in predicting the future! Nevertheless, they were diligent observers. Using only their eyes and, presumably, crude wooden angle-measuring instruments, they were able, among other successes, to work out the length of the year to an accuracy of within 4½ minutes.

Their fellow traders, the Egyptians, continued the tradition of meticulous observation. They knew that when Sirius, the brightest star in the sky, rose just after sunset, the Nile would burst its banks and commence its eagerly awaited annual flood. Their pyramids — colossal monuments to the godlike Pharaohs — were accurately aligned with the north pole of the sky. However, their dogmatic ideas on the structure of the Universe discouraged any observations beyond those which were needed for the practical art of calendar-making.

Early astronomy was thus a cross between timekeeping and astrology. The latter must have grown up as people noticed that certain earthly events, such as the Nile floods, always took place when there was the same configuration of the heavens. Knowing that these configurations occurred regularly, early astronomers must have seemed, to the uninitiated, to be able to peer into the future. If the heavens could affect events, why not the destiny of countries? Of people? Since those days, however, astrology has parted company from astronomy, as astronomers have taken to explaining what is in the sky, and how it moves, as phenomena independent of us on Earth.

The Greeks were the first to put astronomy on a firm scientific footing, which forms the basis of our space-orientated world today. Great thinkers and philosophers, the Greeks were determined to get to grips with the underlying skeleton of any problem. From painstaking observations they constructed a plausible 'model' of a situation which they reasoned from logical principles. This they then tested with further observations. If these fitted the model, all was well; if not, the model was discarded and a new one constructed. Today we call this beautiful and self-consistent procedure 'the scientific method', and all scientists, from astronomers to zoologists, employ it when testing their theories.

The Sun glows redly through the massive uprights of Stonehenge, one of the world's most controversial structures. Most scientists now agree that these monuments were true astronomical observatories, testifying to the sophisticated knowledge of their builders, who lived 5,000 years before us.

The story of Greek astronomy is peppered with legendary names. Pythagoras, the great geometer, was the first to propose (from observation) that the Earth is spherical, not flat, and that it stands still in space. So began the Greek obsession with perfect symmetry. This reached its peak with the philosopher Plato, who was obsessed enough to abandon the scientific method and who taught his pupils not to make any observations at all, as these would be misleading approximations to the perfect truth! Fortunately, his pupils thought otherwise. One of these was Aristotle, whose teachings were to affect the direction of science for more than 1,500 years after his death. He was responsible for putting forward the Greeks' favoured model of the Universe. The Earth is round, he taught, since different stars are visible from different places on the Earth; it is fixed in space, for otherwise the stars would eventually rise in different places; the Sun and planets move around the Earth, but in an extremely complicated way; and all the heavenly bodies are perfect, because no imperfections had been observed at that time. It was a beautiful, self-consistent picture.

Aristotle's ideas had the effect of stimulating observations that would test his theories. Some remarkable feats were achieved. Eratosthenes succeeded in measuring the circumference of the Earth, getting a result almost the same as the best modern measurements. Aristarchus even used a correct, though not very accurate, method to find the distances to the Sun and the Moon. The star maps made by the Greeks were so precise that the Earth's small precessional wobble — a slow shift in the position of the celestial poles — showed up.

As time went by, however, Greece became the scene of political upheaval. The Roman Empire began to make its presence felt. Seven hundred years of science and philosophy shuddered to a halt as the Mediterranean lands erupted in war. During a brief respite in the first century AD, scholars seized their chance to collate the Greek findings in the great Alexandrian library and museum in Egypt. One of these scholars was Claudius Ptolemaeus, usually known as Ptolemy. He collected the essence of Greek astronomy in his great work the Almagest, and luckily for us, he also added to it. Recognizing that the motions of the planets were sometimes unpredictable, he proposed a revolutionary modification to explain them. Each planet, he taught, moves in a wide circle about the Earth, while it pursues smaller loops (epicycles) around this average path. All these loops are circular, because the Greeks believed the circle to be the perfect curve. He went on to predict the positions of the planets for many years into the future.

The future was bleak. Political and re-

above Ptolemy's Earth-centred picture of the cosmos — a synthesis of all the Greek teachings — dominated Man's view of the Universe for as long as 1,500 years, discouraging further exploration. It was not until 1543, when Copernicus suggested that the Earth and planets moved around the Sun, that astronomy began to advance again.

left Mapping the heavens was one of the first tasks of the early astronomers, which they accomplished by joining up the stars into an imaginative array of dot-to-dot patterns or 'constellations'. This much later star chart, compiled by a Dutch Renaissance astronomer, shows the strange objects and fabulous beasts making up the constellations of the Southern Hemisphere skies.

ligious chaos soon plunged the western world into cultural darkness, and the flame of science was extinguished for more than a thousand years.

Even in jumping from Ptolemy's times to 16th century Europe, we miss little of the story of astronomy. Because of the discovery and gradual translation of the old Greek texts, these had become times of great learning and scholarship — except in the field of science. The Church, overwhelmingly dominant in those days, had twisted Aristotle's perfect vision of the Universe into a dogma which offered the supreme proof necessary for the Church's continuing wealth and power. Any challenge to the dogma was tantamount to heresy, and this attitude effectively stultified scientific enquiry.

Rescue came from an unexpected quarter. An elderly Polish monk, Nicolas Copernicus, had become puzzled by the fact that Ptolemy's predicted positions for the planets no longer matched up with reality. To explain the discrepancy, each planet would need to have many more cumbersome epicycles controlling its motions, and Copernicus grew to suspect a major flaw in Ptolemy's model. How much simpler, he mused, if the Sun were to replace the Earth in the centre of the Universe, and the Earth, along with the planets, moved around the Sun.

Copernicus himself did not meet with the wrath of the Church, for he published his suggestion very shortly before he died in 1543. As news gradually spread, the Church authorities became uneasy and a growing wave of interest steadily washed over Europe. Astronomers began to observe the heavens again, instead of relying on the authority of the ancient Greeks. The century that followed saw the first renaissance in astronomy, already mentioned.

The greatest of all these observers was fiery Tycho Brahe, an eccentric Danish nobleman born three years after Copernicus' death. Among other exploits, which included losing his nose in a duel and substituting a replacement allegedly made of gold, Tycho mapped the heavens anew. He recorded the fixed stars and the constantly changing positions of the Sun, the Moon and the planets with a number of astonishingly accurate angle-measuring instruments — quadrants and sextants — which he designed himself. But Tycho was deeply religious and could not bring himself to believe that his observations supported Copernicus' assertions.

His assistant, Johannes Kepler, re-examined the data after Tycho's death. Not only did they back up Copernicus, but also they showed up a still grosser 'imperfection': the planets do not travel around the Sun in perfect circles. Their paths are ovals, or, strictly speaking, ellipses. Kepler incorporated these findings into his three famous Laws of Planetary Motion, which astronomers still invoke when they are concerned with determining the scale and dynamics of the solar system.

Of all the Renaissance astronomers, however, Galileo Galilei is the best-remembered. He was professor of mathe-

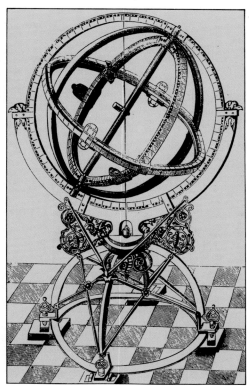

above An armillary sphere, one of the instruments used by the great pre-telescope astronomer Tycho Brahe. Tycho's instruments and his observing skill were second to none, and furnished Kepler, his assistant, with data which would later prove the Earth to be in motion around the Sun.

left Seated before the window of his study, Galileo tests one of his newly-developed 'optic tubes'. Although no better than modern toy telescopes, they helped Galileo make discoveries which ushered in a new era of scientific research.

matics at Padua University when news filtered through of a Dutch invention which used lenses to make distant objects appear closer. Being familiar with lenses, Galileo needed only an outline of the invention to realize how it worked. In 1609 he made his first 'optic tube' and pointed it at the heavens.

Galileo's first telescope was scarcely more than a toy, and magnified only 30 times. Yet with it he saw things that convinced him — and later would convince the world — that Man's view of the Universe had been very wide of the mark. The Moon and the Sun, for example, were not perfect bodies. The Sun showed dark spots, and the Moon appeared pock-marked with craters. Brilliant Venus displayed continuously changing phases as it reflected sunlight, showing without doubt that it circles the Sun and not the Earth. Jupiter was attended by four tiny bodies which revolved around the mighty planet like a miniature solar system.

Fired by his findings and by their support for Copernicus' theory, Galileo rushed into print with dangerously explicit volumes which quickly aroused the wrath of the still-antagonistic Church authorities. After several years of harassment, Galileo was forced to recant.

But all was far from lost. News of Galileo's work rapidly spread to the more enlightened countries of northern Europe, who championed and extended his findings with enthusiasm. Within a few decades both Britain and France had royal observatories dedicated to the dual tasks of refining positional measurements of celestial objects (for the use of navigators on long voyages of discovery) and finding out the nature of the heavenly bodies themselves. As time went by, the hold of the Church weakened still further, and astronomy has never since looked back.

During the intervening years astronomers have built up a picture of the Universe in which its size has grown a hundred trillion-fold and in which our existence has paled utterly into insignificance. Four thousand million humans, along with even greater numbers of plants and animals, populate a small, almost water-covered world which is but one of a family of nine planets. All circle our local star, the Sun.

This solar system of planets is small on the cosmic scale. There is a jump of some 40 million million km (25 million million miles) from the Sun to the nearest star, Alpha Centauri, a distance exceeding the scale of our solar system many thousands of times. The other stars in the sky lie much further from us than Alpha Centauri. Their distances are so vast that miles and kilometres are inadequate to measure them and astronomers must resort to other ways of describing distance.

All the stars we see — and millions too far off to show up even in the world's largest telescopes — belong to a gigantic lens-shaped star island which we call the Milky Way Galaxy. Our Sun is just one average, insignificant star in this multitude of 100,000 million. Beyond, in the depths of space, are similar galaxies stretching into the distance as far as telescopes can probe. If there are a thousand million galaxies — a fairly conservative estimate — then our Universe contains something like 100 million million

million stars. Each of these may have its own family of planets, and among the planets must be some whose surfaces are capable of supporting life.

These are daunting thoughts. We have come a long way, in only four centuries, from our all-important position at the centre of the Universe, to relegation to a minute speck jostling amidst billions of others. Our philosophy has, of necessity, been turned upside down, and it is only natural to feel humble and lost.

We now stand on the threshold of a new era. Until recently our relationship with space was a passive one — although even then our dealings were exceedingly fruitful, for they generated almost all our ideas about the structure and framework of the Universe we inhabit. Today we are beginning actively to interact with the worlds beyond. We are starting to sever the links with planet Earth and see ourselves as citizens of the Universe. Who can tell what changes this new renaissance will bring? Will we even recognize ourselves after the passage of another four centuries?

left *The Moon, our nearest neighbour and companion world in space. Men have roamed her barren plains and scaled her rugged peaks, but in doing so, they have explored only a very tiny corner of the Universe. Even the closest star is a hundred million times farther away than the Moon.*

far left *A dying star. This former celestial beacon has gently puffed away its outer layers into space. Our Sun is just one average star out of 100 thousand million which make up our local star island, the Galaxy. The Sun, too, may eventually end its life like this.*

above *At 2¼ million lightyears away, the Andromeda Galaxy is the most remote object that can be seen with the unaided eye. It is visible in Autumn skies as a dimly-glowing patch, but telescopes reveal it as a close star-island, similar to — and even larger than — our own. Stars scattered over the photograph are nearby members of our own Galaxy.*

EYES ON THE UNIVERSE

Even if Man does reach the stars, astronomers will not be in any hurry to abandon their telescopes. The Universe is so vast that there will always be worlds beyond Man's direct reach, and it is unlikely that even the nearest galaxies will be visited by a boarding-party from Earth, except in the inconceivably remote future. For the time being, the new and the old astronomy will continue to develop together.

Anyone visiting a modern observatory, with its remote-controlled computer-driven telescopes and the bewildering arrays of attachments, might well think it a scene from 'astronomy new' rather than 'astronomy old'. Yet such an institution is essentially a scaled-up version of Galileo's first tiny telescope, in the same way that his instrument was a more powerful version of the human eye. For all their apparent complexity, telescopes are simply giant collectors of light. The bigger their light-collecting area, the fainter the objects they can show us and the more information we can glean.

Admittedly, modern telescopes do not bear much resemblance to Galileo's 'optic tube'. Galileo's instrument collected light with a lens at the front end, and the image formed by it was magnified by another, the eyepiece, through which the observer

looked. However, lenses have an unfortunate property of spreading out light into its constituent colours — just as raindrops disperse sunlight into a rainbow — and, try as they might, the early observers could not entirely eradicate the stray colours caused by the main lens. It took a genius of the calibre of Sir Isaac Newton to solve the problem, by adopting a completely different approach.

Newton designed a telescope which collected and focused light with a concave curved mirror, rather like a modern shaving mirror; as before, the image was magnified with an eyepiece lens. He displayed this new telescope at the Royal Society in 1672, and gradually astronomers began to forsake their refracting telescopes — or 'refractors' — for 'reflectors'.

Both types of telescope have their roles to play in modern astronomy. The world's biggest refractor, at the Yerkes Observatory in Wisconsin, has a lens 102 cm (40 inches) in diameter and was built as long ago as 1897. In general, the stability of refractors makes them excellent for measuring precise positions of objects in programmes lasting for several years or decades, such as charting the course of a star through space ('proper motion') or the minuscule wobble superimposed on a star's motion by the

above *Delicate wisps and streamers of gas framing the Orion Nebula are captured in this photograph by amateur astronomer Ron Arbour. With the right equipment and sufficient experience, amateurs can take photographs rivalling those of professionals in their detail and beauty. Arbour uses a 21.6 cm (8½ inch) diameter home-built reflecting telescope near Southampton, England.*

right *Forks of summer lightning dramatically illuminate the clustered domes of Kitt Peak National Observatory in Arizona, USA. It boasts the largest single collection of astronomical instruments in the world, and like most professional observatories, it is a national facility open to all astronomers. Its largest instrument is a 4 metre (158 inch) reflector which was first brought into use in 1973.*

presence of orbiting planets. Today, however, most astronomy research programmes concentrate on determining the nature of extremely distant, and therefore exceedingly faint, objects. Thus the astronomer's cry is always for 'more light', and reflectors are more efficient at collecting light than refractors. Add to this the fact that large mirrors are considerably easier to manufacture than big lenses, and that the path of the light in reflecting telescopes can be 'folded' by suitable mirror arrangements to make these instruments more compact, and it becomes clear why nowadays the majority of the world's most important telescopes are reflectors.

The mightiest of these giants is the Russian 6 metre (236 inch) telescope at the Zelenchukskaya Astrophysical Observatory in the Caucasus Mountains — the size refers

Left *On a peak near Zelenchuk in the Caucasus Mountains stands the world's largest optical telescope — the Soviet 6 metre (236 inch) reflector. Its huge dome, seen here with the slit open preparatory to a night's observing, is 53 metres (174 feet) high — nearly half the height of the giant Saturn V Moon-rocket.*

above *The new Anglo-Australian telescope at Siding Spring near Sydney, Australia. This 3.9 metre (153 inch) reflector has been described by its British and Australian users as "the best in the world".*

to the huge mirror, nearly 20 feet across. For two decades before the completion of the Russian telescope, the 'world's largest' title was held by the famous 5 metre (200 inch) reflector of the Hale Observatories on Palomar Mountain, California, USA, which, in turn, succeeded the 2.5 metre (100 inch) reflector on nearby Mount Wilson. Britain's biggest will be the 4.2 metre (165 inch) William Herschel Telescope, soon to take its place on the UK's new observatory on La Palma, in the Canary Islands. Together with the 2.5 metre (100 inch) Isaac Newton Telescope, and the smaller 1 metre (40 inch), it will be operated by remote control via telephone lines from the Royal Greenwich Observatory in Sussex.

New observatories have been springing up worldwide. Those at La Silla, in Chile, and Siding Spring, Australia, scour the virgin skies of the southern hemisphere; while the telescopes on Mauna Kea, Hawaii, are nearest of all to heaven — 4200 metres (14,000 feet) above the polluted atmosphere at sea level. Their telescopes, contrary to popular image, seldom take pictures — one result of the takeover of astronomy by microchip technology.

Until this revolution occurred, most telescopes worked as enormous cameras, taking long-exposure photographs of faint objects. The images on the photographic plates were studied and measured up later. Part of the astronomer's job was to ensure that the telescope accurately tracked the object across the wheeling sky, constantly correcting for tiny changes in its position caused by currents in the Earth's atmosphere. As these exposures could run into several hours, in an open dome left unheated to prevent air currents, it is easy to see how the image of the eccentric astronomer originated! However, even though photographic plates are far better than the human eye in recording and storing the elusive light from faint objects, they are only 1 per cent efficient — 99 per cent of the light falling on to a plate goes to waste.

It was the behaviour of light itself which ushered in the new breed of detectors. These make use of the *photoelectric effect*, whose explanation early this century earned Albert Einstein the Nobel Prize. Einstein showed how light, on hitting certain metals such as rubidium or caesium, causes electrons to be ejected from their surfaces. The more intense the beam of light, the more electrons are knocked out. Because a stream of electrons is just an electric current, it is an easy matter to find out how much light is hitting the metal surface by measuring the size of the resulting current.

The first photoelectric device used by astronomers was the *photomultiplier tube*, whose highly amplified current, made by 'multiplying' electrons in a cascade within a valve-like tube, could measure star brightnesses very accurately. Astronomers gradually learned the trick of focusing the electron beams with magnetic fields, so that an intensely amplified image of the body under observation could be built up. Because highly energetic electrons (instead

of light) form the photographic image, the process is far more efficient. Such an *image intensifier* — the 'Spectracon' is an early and much-used example — is as sensitive on a 50 cm (20 inch) telescope as is the 5 metre (200 inch) Hale telescope equipped with photographic plates.

These new detectors have cut exposure times from hours to minutes, lessening the need for extremely large telescopes. At the same time, they have ushered in an aston-

top *A new concept in cheap telescope design — the Multiple Mirror Telescope. Perched 2,600 metres (8,500 ft) atop Mt Hopkins, Arizona, its six 1.8 metre (72 inch) mirrors have the light-gathering capacity of a 4.5 metre (176 inch) instrument, making this the third largest telescope in the world. It is specially designed for use at infrared wavelengths.*

above *The control panel of the Anglo-Australian Telescope rivals that of an aircraft in its complexity. Such precise equipment is essential to fix the huge instrument on a flickering spot of light and then track it with hairsbreadth accuracy as Earth spins underneath. The task would be virtually impossible without computer control.*

right *An astronomer's-eye view of the famous Hale 5 metre (200 inch) reflector on Palomar Mountain. Photographed from the observing floor, the picture reveals complex detection equipment attached to the Cassegrain focus behind the main mirror. Until recently, this was the world's largest telescope, and it is exceeded only by the Russian 6 metre.*

ishing array of devices which work in an ultrasensitive television camera mode, commanded by built-in minicomputers, with as many variations as there are astronomers designing them. Today's optical astronomer now has extraordinary flexibility at the telescope (or, more accurately, in the warm, air-conditioned control room) to get the precise information he needs about any astronomical object. Photography still goes on, particularly in studying very large areas of sky which cannot, as yet, be covered by the new detectors. Help is usually at hand, however, in the form of computer-driven telescopes, automatic guiding, fast-response photographic plates and automated analysis at a later stage.

Most of the new detectors, however, do not spend their lives taking celestial snapshots. Their task is to record faint fragments of *dispersed* light, which after being gathered by the telescope has passed through another indispensable weapon in the astronomer's armoury — the *spectroscope*. Here the colour-producing property of lenses, which caused so many problems for the early observers, has been turned to spectacular advantage. Light is a wave motion, composed of a whole series of electromagnetic vibrations. The refractive property of glass, seen to best effect in a prism, spreads out light into its constituent wavelengths, which we perceive as a rainbow of colours. The *spectrum* so produced ranges from short-wavelength blue (400 nm) up to long-wavelength red (700 nm); although 'long' is a relative term when we consider that 1 nm (nanometre) measures only a millionth of a millimetre!

Light coming from any source — such as an incandescent gas — can be spread out by a prism, but modern scientists (whether in a physics laboratory or an astronomical observatory) prefer to disperse light with a *diffraction grating*, somewhat similar to a whole series of tiny prisms but absorbing less light. A spectroscopist examining gas spectra works rather like a detective analysing fingerprints. Each chemical element has a different spectrum, as the atoms comprising a gas of that element produce light only at very specific wavelengths ('spectral lines'). By looking at the spectral lines in the spectrum of light coming from a planet, a star or a galaxy, astronomers can tell a great deal about its make-up — what kind of gases it contains, its temperature, whether the gases are

constricted by strong pressure or magnetic fields, and even how fast it is moving. Spectroscopy is truly the key which, during the past century, has unlocked the secrets of the stars.

Although light waves seem so important to the astronomer, they are only one tiny part — a thousand million million millionth part — of a band of electromagnetic vibrations of different wavelengths. These range from ultrashort gamma and X-rays,

through ultraviolet radiation and visible light, up to the very-long-wavelength infrared radiation and radio waves. Light assumes such importance because our atmosphere is transparent to it (and because our eyes can detect it). Shorter radiations, which are damaging to living tissue, are fortunately absorbed high above the Earth's surface, as are the very long radio waves and, to some extent, the infrared. Radio waves with wavelengths

A fading sunset highlights the massive 76 metre (250 foot) Mk Ia radio telescope at Jodrell Bank, Cheshire, UK. Instruments like this are specially designed to detect radio waves from space, but they register radio interference from Earth too. Leakage from microwave ovens has become a serious problem.

inset *'Radio photograph' of the Milky Way, synthesized from half a million observations by the 26 metre (86 foot) radio telescope at Hat Creek, California, USA. The telescope was tuned in to radiation coming from cold hydrogen gas in space, and the colours — blue for approach, red for recession — show the gas to be in a state of continual motion.*

between 1 cm and 30 metres, however, can reach ground. During the past 50 years astronomers have been able to explore virtually the whole range of the electromagnetic spectrum, which has enabled them to pinpoint the natural processes operating in astronomical objects which give rise to the different radiations.

On first sight, the great steel dishes of the radio astronomer seem to have little in common with the instruments in the optical observatory. But look again: the dish works like a huge reflecting telescope, focusing the waves on to an aerial, whence an electrical signal travels to a receiver to be amplified before being directly recorded on computer tape. The computer can analyse the results — produced as either a string of numbers, maps or even processed 'radio photographs' — in a fraction of the time taken by a human researcher. Ever since radio astronomy grew up after World War II (although Karl Jansky first detected radio waves from space in 1931), its adherents have enthusiastically embraced the latest in computer technology and electronics. This spirit has now fed back, with great effect, to the new generation of optical astronomers.

Detecting radio waves from the natural transmitters in space — wrecks of stars, exploding galaxies and sizzling planets — has never been easy. The total amount of energy in radio waves received by all the

right 'Photograph' of X-rays from the Crab Nebula by the orbiting Einstein Observatory — a satellite launched in November 1978 to survey the high-energy heavens. X-rays are produced by objects which are very hot or extremely energetic. The Crab Nebula is the remains of a star which was seen to explode over 900 years ago.

below High above Earth's turbulent atmosphere, the Space Telescope, launched and maintained by Space Shuttle crews, makes its observations. With its 2.4 metre (95 inch) mirror, this telescope — scheduled for launch in the late 1980s — will see farther into the depths of space than any other. Astronomers confidently predict that it will create a host of new problems for them to solve.

below right The face of our Sun, one of the few astronomical bodies for which lack of light is no problem. The glaring, churning sea of gases which makes up its visible surface is at a temperature of 5,500°C; the slightly cooler sunspot appears dark by comparison. The Sun emits powerfully at most other wavelengths too, from X-rays to radio waves. X-ray satellites in particular are revealing much about solar radiations which do not penetrate our atmosphere.

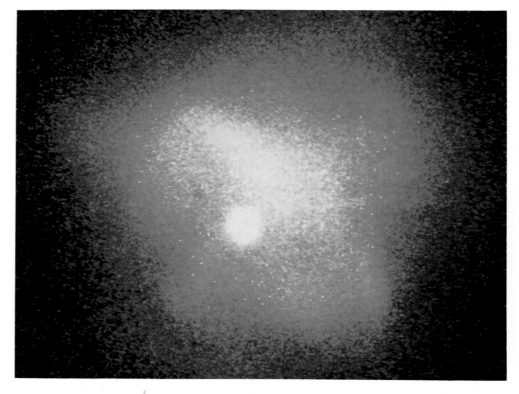

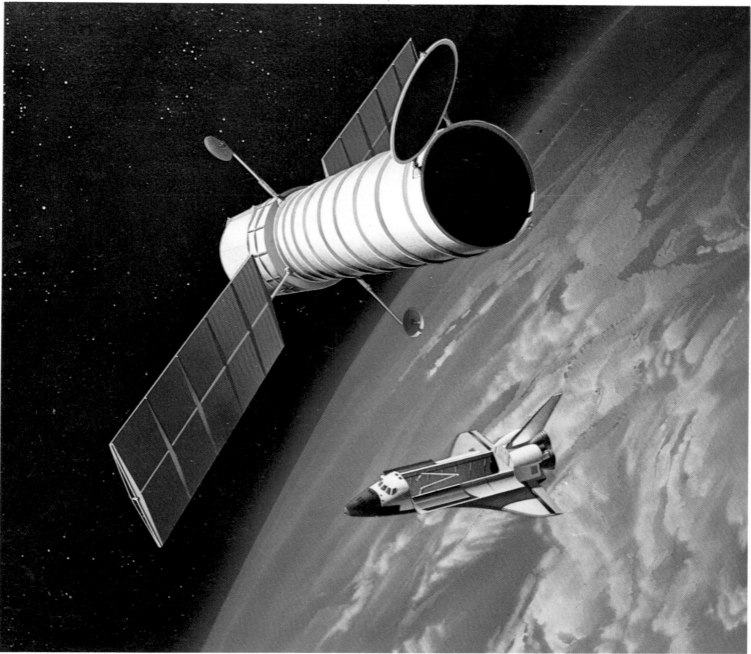

radio telescopes on Earth, and added up over the entire history of radio astronomy, is less than would be expended in picking up a feather. Radio astronomers have had to become adept at suppressing spurious radio 'noise' — and that means interference from nearby traffic and microwave ovens too! The other fundamental limitation concerns the long wavelength of the radio waves. Optical telescopes have very large mirrors compared with the length of the light waves, which means they can see very fine details — they have very high 'resolution'. However, structural considerations preclude the building of a radio telescope with the same ratio of wavelength to diameter, for it would have to be several kilometres across!

Former Astronomer Royal, Sir Martin Ryle, whose favourite weather is the dank fenland fog, ideal for radio astronomy, has pioneered an ingenious solution to this problem. By a technique called aperture synthesis he and his team at Cambridge electronically link the output from a line of radio telescopes and allow the Earth's rotation to swing them round as they follow a source. By stacking the results in a computer and changing the spacing of the dishes each day, Ryle is able to synthesize a radio telescope the equivalent of 5 km across, capable of resolving detail as fine as can be seen in an optical telescope. A similar technique, rejoicing in the name of 'Very Long Baseline Interferometry', links up radio telescopes thousands of miles apart (sometimes situated on opposite sides of the world) to 'see' even finer structure in radio sources.

Between the wavelengths of radio waves and light is infrared radiation, emitted by 'lukewarm' bodies in space — planets, forming stars, gas clouds, dust grains. It's best observed from space, and scientists are still getting to grips with the thousands of discoveries made by the first Infrared Astronomy Satellite IRAS, which orbited Earth during 1983. These will be followed up at infrared observatories throughout the world — placed as high as possible to get above the water vapour — before astronomers plan the next space mission. In particular, they hope to learn for certain how stars and planets are born.

The 'shortest wavelength' astronomers are well used to nailbiting satellite launches. Failure means the end of many years' work in designing tiny experimental packages which have vied for valuable space aboard a satellite; success will guarantee data, often totally unexpected, telling of the weird nature of the high-energy heavens. Gamma-ray, X-ray and ultraviolet astronomers share similar problems, as they need to send their detectors high above Earth's absorbing atmosphere. Until 1970, when Uhuru, the first X-ray detecting satellite, was launched, the total flight time spent on brief rocket forays could be measured in minutes. Now many satellites, including Exosat, the Einstein Observatory and the International Ultraviolet Explorer, have surveyed the sky at these wavelengths. Many use gas-filled tubes, such as Geiger counters, and sensitive direction-finding collimators to locate flaring stars, active galaxies — and even perhaps black holes.

The end of this chapter finds us back once again with the optical astronomers. This time they are poised on the brink of a new and great adventure, one which is certain to set up repercussions throughout the whole world of astronomy. Late in 1986 or, more likely, in early 1987, the Space Shuttle will jettison the Space Telescope into an orbit 500 km (300 miles) above the Earth. This 2.4 metre (95 inch) instrument will be the first to escape above the grey churning atmosphere of our planet. The blackness of the airless skies will mean that the Space Telescope can pick up objects more than 100 times fainter than those that are reached by telescopes on Earth — about 1,000 million times fainter than the unaided human eye can see. Correspondingly, we will be able to look further into the depths of space. Since light does not travel instantaneously fast, this means that we are seeing back in time, so far back that the Space Telescope will show us objects in the very first stages of their evolution.

In the absence of our heaving atmosphere, which continuously distorts and changes the positions and appearance of objects in the sky, the Space Telescope will be able to ascertain the whereabouts of stars to an accuracy ten times better than that which we can achieve on Earth. Positional astronomers are already rejoicing at the prospect of measuring distances in space more accurately, as well as recognizing the opportunities offered to detect planets around other stars. The Space Telescope has the extra advantage that, unlike the X-ray instruments, it will not be entirely remote-controlled. Manned missions in Space Shuttle will regularly repair and maintain it, bringing it back to Earth should all not be well.

This brings us on to the future of Man in space. . . .

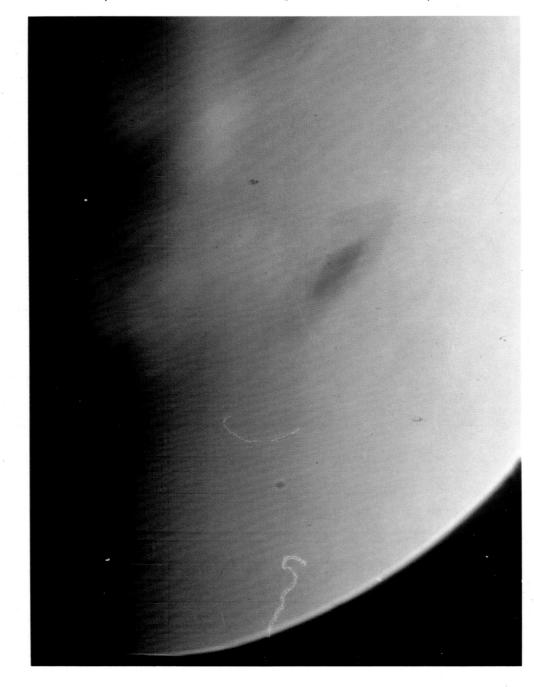

MAN CONQUERS SPACE

Less than five years after Britain's Astronomer Royal had dismissed the possibility of space travel as 'utter bilge', a farmer's son was circling our planet more than 200 km (125 miles) up. On 12 April 1961 at 06.07 GMT, Flight Major Yuri Gagarin, at the age of 27, was launched into space. While the astonished world watched, Gagarin made one circuit of the globe in his tiny Vostok 1 spacecraft, and landed safely near a small village, his reentry capsule slowed by parachutes. In 108 minutes he had travelled more than 40,000 km (25,000 miles).

Only 3½ years before, the Russians had begun to shake the world with their daring space exploits. Then it was with the launch of Sputnik 1, the first-ever spacecraft. This 58 cm (23 inch) aluminium sphere, which bleeped its way around the Earth every 96 minutes, was tiny by present standards; yet with a weight of 83.6 kg (184 lb) it was 74.1 kg (163 lb) heavier than the satellite which America was preparing to launch the following year.

Within a month Sputnik 1 had been joined by the considerably heavier Sputnik 2. Both craft circled the Earth along with the rockets which had boosted them into orbit, gleaming like stars in the reflected sunlight to their millions of delighted watchers below. Sputnik 2 carried a passenger — a lovely female dog named Laika. Although Laika was automatically fed and watered, the Russians had no plans for the capsule's safe return, and so allowed the dog to die as she used up her air supply. It was a kinder death than that suffered by her craft as it was consumed by friction on plummeting back into Earth's atmosphere 5½ months later.

Many more experiments with dogs, plants, insects and dummy cosmonauts followed, to evaluate the effects of space on living beings and test safe methods of reentry to the atmosphere. Gagarin's flight, however, was none the less a shock when it happened — except to a few journalists who had picked up rumours (false, as it turned out) just beforehand. Partly because of the secrecy imposed by the cold war, and also because events were happening so rapidly, no one could believe that the Russians were so far ahead. The Russians left no doubt. In the two years following Gagarin's flight five cosmonauts, one a woman, had made safe flights lasting up to five days in the 2.3 metre (7½ foot) diameter Vostok capsule. Some of their flights were simultaneous, the object being to achieve a close rendezvous of less than a few kilometres between the two spacecraft. Already, it appeared, the Russians were concentrating on the techniques necessary to build space stations.

America's initial attempts at manned spaceflight looked puny by comparison.

Alan Shepard's first brief sortie into space, on 5 May 1961, was not even an orbit — just a 15½ minute jump in his Mercury capsule to a height of 187 km (117 miles). Yet only three weeks later, the late President Kennedy was addressing Congress with the words: 'I believe that this nation should commit itself to achieving the goal, before the decade is out, of landing a man on the Moon and returning him safely to Earth'. And, amazingly, they did it — in just over eight years.

Those years between Kennedy's commitment and Neil Armstrong's reassuring 'Houston, Tranquillity Base here. The Eagle has landed' were fraught, and sometimes foolhardy ones for the National Aeronautics and Space Administration (NASA). When Kennedy made his pledge, the part of Houston destined to become Mission Control, the nerve centre of the manned space enterprise, was just a vast tract of marshland. Thus, in its haste to bring the president's words to fulfilment, NASA cut corners (to be fair, the Russians must have done so too).

America's first orbital flight, on 20 February 1962, was a tribute to man rather than machine. A technical fault caused a great deal of the Mercury capsule's heatshield to disintegrate, and led astronaut John Glenn to believe that he faced certain fiery death on returning to Earth after a premature three orbits. Yet throughout he reacted calmly, and eventually made a safe reentry, to splash down in the Atlantic Ocean — sea retrievals being standard American practice — just off Puerto Rico. Subsequent flights

above   *Yuri Gagarin, first man in space. Sadly, it was to be his only trip: he was killed in a plane crash on 27 March 1968 while training for another space mission.*

right   *Astronaut Buzz Aldrin sets up an aluminium foil detector on the Moon's surface to collect charged particles streaming from the Sun. Behind him is Eagle, the Apollo 11 mission's Lunar Module, first manned craft to touch down on another world.*

were more successful and the Mercury astronauts were allowed far more control of their craft than were their Soviet counterparts. However, they still badly lacked their opposite numbers' man-hours in space.

Between March 1965 and November 1966 this situation dramatically reversed. With the launching of ten craft of the Gemini series (Geminis 1 and 2 being earlier unmanned missions), the astronauts logged a grand total of 28 million km (17½ million miles) travelled in space; the cosmonauts' total stood at 12 million km (7½ million miles). In their roomier two-man craft the Gemini astronauts practised close approaches and, later, docking between space vehicles — a technique essential for the success of the lunar mission. By long-duration flights and in extravehicular 'space walks' (first pioneered by cosmonaut Alexei Leonov from his Voskhod 2 capsule on 18 March 1965) they tested the effects of space on the human body and gave it the 'all clear'. The road to the Moon now looked wide open.

NASA had already begun testing their Apollo mooncraft and were developing the enormous Saturn 5 launcher which would provide the 3,400 tonne (7½ million lb) thrust necessary to get three men and a lander craft to the Moon. All seemed set fair for the first manned launching on 27 January 1967, scheduled as a suborbital flight to test the Apollo systems. It was not to be. During a simulated countdown astronauts Virgil Grissom, veteran of two flights, Edward White, first American space-walker, and Roger Chaffee perished in a sudden fire fanned by the cabin's pure oxygen atmosphere. No more Americans flew in space for nearly two years. Only three months later the Russians suffered their first space tragedy, as their new long-endurance craft Soyuz 1 plummeted to Earth in a tangle of parachute wires, killing cosmonaut Vladimir Komarov. For both nations it was a time of mourning, and of reappraisal.

In view of these circumstances, the American space comeback seemed all the more audacious. Christmas 1968 found Frank Borman, James Lovell and William Anders circling the Moon ten times in Apollo 8. Swooping to within 111 km (69 miles) of the bleak lunar surface, they convinced the TV-goggling world and the Russian space scientists too that the Moon was clearly within their grasp. A few months later the goal was achieved.

On 21 July 1969 astronaut Neil Armstrong became the first human being to embrace

Rehearsal for Moon-landing: astronaut David Scott, pilot of the command Module Gumdrop on the Apollo 9 mission, undertakes EVA — Extra-Vehicular Activity — above the Mississippi valley. The first manned lunar landing was preceded by four manned 'test flights' like this, two of which (Apollos 8 and 10) took place around the Moon.

another world, with the oft-misquoted words 'That's one small step for (a) man, one giant leap for mankind'. But the first lunar landing, made in the Eagle landing craft, had not been easy. A navigational error had been fed to Eagle's computer, and the two-man crew did not know their position until the last few moments before landing — when they had only 30 seconds' worth of fuel left! Armstrong, attempting to juggle fuel, forward velocity and down velocity, finally brought Eagle down in a sequence exactly like that in the 'Lunar Landing' minicomputer game that many of us play, often unsuccessfully, just for fun.

Armstrong and fellow astronaut Edwin 'Buzz' Aldrin spent almost a day on the Moon, setting up instruments and collecting 20.8 kg (46 lb) of rock samples before blasting off to dock with their colleague Mike Collins in Moon-orbiting command module Columbia. The three returned to a heroes' welcome — and the world scarcely noticed that the unmanned Russian Luna 15 craft, sent to the Moon at exactly the same time, had crashed, failing in its mission to return rock samples without the complexity and danger of a manned mission.

Four months later, still before Kennedy's decade was out, Apollo 12 went the way of its predecessor and made a landing of pinpoint accuracy within a few hundred metres of the long-defunct Surveyor 3 robot probe, parts of which the astronauts returned to Earth. With the placing of the nuclear-powered Apollo Lunar Surface Experiments Package (ALSEP) on the Moon for continuous monitoring of the environment, Apollo 12 became the first truly scientific, as opposed to political, Moon mission.

With Kennedy's pledge fulfilled four times over, and with an avalanche of data flooding back to Earth to satisfy the clamouring scientists, America's luck was in. Or was it? Not only the superstitious worried about Apollo 13.

Launched on 11 April 1970, the craft was intended to carry its crew of James Lovell and Fred Haise, assisted by command module pilot John Swigert, to Fra Mauro, a dangerous highland area of the Moon. Two days later, with the craft more than three-quarters of the way to its destination, there was an explosion. It was followed by an immediate loss of electrical power. The astronauts were in utmost peril: they had only meagre power to manoeuvre and just a couple of days' supply of oxygen left. It transpired later that a short-circuit had caused an oxygen tank in the service module to explode, blowing out a 4 by 1.8 metre (13 by 6 foot) access door in the process. To survive, the astronauts had but one alternative. They had to transfer to the cramped lunar module, stored below their command module living quarters, and rely on its independent supplies of life-giving air and power.

Although there was no question of a landing taking place, the craft was still on a trajectory which took it behind the Moon. Despite the fact that they might never get home again, Haise and Swigert spent the time enthusiastically snapping the lunar far-side, obtaining some of the best pictures ever taken. Lovell, clearly feeling the strain, was told: 'You've been here before, we haven't' — this referring to his earlier trip on Apollo 8.

Amazingly, Apollo 13 returned to Earth safely, after the three astronauts reoccupied the command module, the only part of the craft with a heatshield, and reentered the atmosphere under its final residue of power. The rescue had taken teams of NASA scientists working in long shifts around the clock; it had needed completely reworked computer data; and it had required calmness, cooperation and courage from the three astronauts. NASA, learning from its mistakes, at once modified the design of the Apollo craft.

Four more Apollos flew. Apollo 14 investigated the Fra Mauro uplands where 13 had been destined to go. Apollos 15, 16 and 17 made extensive use of a lunar rover in which the astronauts ranged across the surface at 11 km per hour (7 miles per hour)

above 'The picture of the century' — Buzz Aldrin poses for photographer Neil Armstrong (seen reflected in Aldrin's visor) on the occasion of the first manned lunar landing in Apollo 11. Aldrin's 'Moonsuit', together with the backpack, weighed more than he did and cost $100,000 (£42,000).

right Science on the Moon: an astronaut sets up experiment packages between the Apollo 12 Lunar Module and a radio aerial. This mission returned to Earth carrying parts of the long-dead Surveyor 3 probe and a quantity of lunar rock samples for examination in the laboratory.

and picked up greater quantities of rock samples. As one astronaut put it, these were the real 'superscientific' missions.

As if to reinforce this, the last Apollo mission carried geologist Harrison 'Jack' Schmitt as a crew member, countering criticisms that NASA never flew qualified research scientists. Schmitt's euphoria on reaching the steep-sided Taurus-Littrow valley was a joy to behold: continuously running television cameras showed him stumbling and bouncing over the lunar terrain, singing a garbled version of a popular song — 'I was strolling on the Moon one day . . . in the merry merry month of . . . December'.

Apollo 17, at 12 days and 14 hours the longest-ever lunar mission, splashed down on 17 December 1972 with its three crew and a record 116.5 kg (257 lb) of lunar rocks. But Apollo was over, after only three years of manned lunar exploration. NASA was battling against deep budget cuts, and the Soviet space challenge had subsided. At this point space seemed to lose a lot of its life and colour.

Now that the excitement of getting men to the Moon had died down, it was time to turn to practicalities. Medical tests showed that astronauts could live quite happily for short periods in space conditions — but could the human body adapt to long-duration flights, such as journeys to the planets? To find out, the Americans had to reorientate their space programme and follow the Russian direction in building space stations for long-term visits.

Skylab, launched without crew on 14 May 1973, was — at 75 tonnes — the heaviest

object ever put into orbit, some four times the weight of the Salyut space stations which the Russians were testing. The new era of 'space on a shoestring' decreed that Skylab be made as cheaply as possible, so NASA simply converted the third stage of a massive Saturn 5 rocket to make the shell of the craft. Inside were roomy laboratories, workshops and living quarters which awaited the arrival of three-man crews from Earth.

Reaching the space station eleven days later, the first three space dwellers had more to cope with than they had bargained for. Skylab was badly crippled. Only a minute after launch one of the solar panels (which provided electrical power) had been destroyed and the other jammed as a white-painted meteoroid shield accidentally tore off. As a result, the underpowered space-craft had severely overheated. The crew spent their 28 days in space (a record at that time) patching up the damaged space station by erecting a parasol sunshade and unjamming the other panel — both difficult operations which needed several hours' work outside the spacecraft. Despite these exertions, the three men returned to Earth remarkably fit and well.

Before the year was out, Skylab had become a temporary home to two further crews. Each beat its predecessor's endurance record, spending the time making observations of Earth, Sun and sky, and performing experiments which were especially suited to space conditions. Skylab's last crew logged a record 84 days — almost three months — in space.

The missions over, Skylab remained empty. Scientists expected that it would remain in orbit 435 km (270 miles) above the Earth until the early 1980s, when the slight but perpetual friction with the uppermost tenuous layers of the atmosphere would drag it down into successively lower orbits. In these denser layers friction would be greater, and eventually the space station would be slowed so much that it could not stay in orbit. Skylab would plummet back to Earth, showering unfortunate countries beneath with chunks of fiery debris.

NASA scientists, however, were confident that Skylab would not suffer this dreadful fate. One of the first tasks allocated to the Space Shuttle, originally scheduled to fly in mid-1979, was to nose Skylab to a higher, safer orbit. But things didn't work out that way.

To begin with, Shuttle was delayed. Then an unexpectedly early burst of activity from the Sun, which was approaching its eleven-yearly maximum of activity, expanded Earth's atmosphere, so increasing the air resistance on Skylab and causing its orbit to decay far more rapidly than predicted. By the beginning of 1979 everyone knew that Skylab was going to fall. The problem was that no one knew where.

Even NASA scientists were in the dark until the last few orbits. All they could do then was to issue commands which changed the attitude of the doomed

spacecraft — turning it broadside-on to slow it, end-on to reduce air drag — to prevent it from falling on to a populated country. Although they expected that most of the craft would burn up on reentry, there were some large chunks of metal, notably a 2⅓ tonne (5100 lb) airlock shroud and a 1¾ tonne (3900 lb) lead-lined film vault, which were certain to hit ground.

It happened on 11 July 1979. Fortunately, the scientists were successful. Residents of Western Australia were treated to a spectacular fireworks display of red and blue man-made 'meteors' as Skylab plunged harmlessly into the ocean in hundreds of molten fragments. The following day the barren deserts inland were invaded by scores of treasure hunters, lured by NASA's attractive financial rewards to send back the few chunks which had come down on land.

left *Into space: an Atlas-Centaur 40 rocket launches a Comstar D2 communications satellite into Earth orbit. The Atlas launcher is an improved and modified version of an American intercontinental military missile which first flew in 1957, and it is now used extensively for putting medium payloads into orbit.*

above *A model of a Soviet Vostok spacecraft — which carried the first man into space — dominates the permanent space exhibition in Moscow. At right, a Soviet Cosmos launcher is flanked by a dramatic photograph of a cosmonaut spacewalking.*

Skylab apart, spacecraft and debris fall to Earth more frequently than most people realize. The majority of fragments are small and, like meteorites, end up safely in the sea or on uninhabited parts of the Earth. However, accidents do happen. Early in 1978 a Russian satellite fell on a deserted region of Canada. Like a couple of dozen other satellites in orbit today, Cosmos 954 was powered by a nuclear device, and this led to widespread fears about possible radiation hazards that the crash might have caused. At least four other nuclear-powered satellites are known to have crashed to Earth previously. Furthermore, Soviet space scientists routinely allow their Salyut space stations to 'undergo orbital decay' when their job is done.

However, the Salyut craft, at 12 metres (39 feet) in length and 18½ tonnes in weight, are only a quarter the size of America's Skylab and present correspondingly less danger as they reenter. Since 1971 the Russians have concentrated their manned space efforts on developing these two-man space laboratories. Crews travel up to the stations in Soyuz spacecraft, which also ferry supplies and food to the cosmonauts. Since the programme started, the Russians have concentrated on flights of successively longer duration. The current world record-holders are Valentin Lebedev and Anatoli Berezovoy, who spent 211 days aboard Salyut 7 in 1982. However, such long flights in space have their drawbacks. Lebedev's diary, written in the cramped quarters of the spacecraft, describes the period as one of great strain, when he pined for his home and family.

With the trend towards longer flights, space authorities in both Russia and America have grown aware of the increased need for efficient rescue facilities should space-farers of either nation run into difficulties. Before 1975, however, rescue of the crew of a stricken American craft by a Soviet ship, or vice versa, would have been impossible. Crew on Russia's everyday Soyuz craft breathed ordinary air at normal pressure; their American counterparts on Apollo inhaled pure oxygen at one-third the pressure. Were an astronaut in those days to crawl through a Russian hatch, he would have suffered a severe case of 'the bends' — but even this would have been im-

The Skylab saga: above, a Saturn V launcher puts Skylab into Earth orbit on 15 May 1973. Seconds after this photograph was taken, the vicious air drag ripped off the micrometeorite shield, destroying one solar panel and jamming the other. The craft, soon to be occupied by its first crew, was without power and dangerously overheating. Experts back on Earth studied secret spy satellite pictures of the space station (such as that shown on the right, with the solar panel — lower left — seen jammed shut) before deciding on a course of action. The result is shown in the top picture: astronauts Conrad and Kerwin freed the panel with pruning shears and erected a replacement sunshield to cool the stricken spacecraft.

possible, as the docking arrangements were completely incompatible.

The Apollo-Soyuz Test Project (ASTP) set out to remedy these deficiencies. For several years Soviet and American teams worked closely together in each other's countries, modifying their craft so that they would be able to dock together and exchange crews. Engineers spent the time designing a special airlock system, while the crews (and their back-ups) familiarized themselves with their opposite numbers' craft and language. The mission was an outstanding success. On 17 July 1975 Thomas Stafford and Donald 'Deke' Slayton crawled from their Apollo craft, docked nose-to-nose with Soyuz 19, to be greeted by veteran cosmonaut Alexei Leonov and his colleague Valeri Kubasov. The four shared a celebratory Russian meal before getting down to two days of experiments while their craft were docked.

Many commentators have protested that the motivation behind ASTP was entirely political. However, they overlook the fact that we now have a rescue facility — a safety net in space. There is also the capability of building a vast international space station, made and manned by staff from many nations; and since ASTP all manned spacecraft, present and future, must have compatible docking mechanisms and be capable of transferring crews.

Space is no respecter of nationalities. All space travellers have had the same conditions to bear, the same problems to face. The severity of some of these situations, and the rigorous training needed in order to face them, is reflected in the high dropout rate of the astronaut corps — among men selected for their supposedly almost superhuman qualities. By now most of the Apollo astronauts have left NASA. Neil Armstrong is Professor of Astronautical Engineering at Cincinnati University and Jack Schmitt is a senator. Apollo 15's James Irwin has since turned to evangelism, while America's first man in space, Alan Shepard, now sells beer for a living.

To begin with, even the NASA administrators were not sure quite what they required of their astronauts. At the dawning of the space programme a kind of superman image was all-important, and so the trainee astronauts cooperated, in a rather tongue-in-cheek manner. Some of the early trials involved the astronauts' responses to Rorschach (ink-blot) tests. Word quickly got around that chances of selection were higher if the subject demonstrated his manly drive by seeing parts of the female anatomy in the ink-blot patterns!

The early spacemen were mainly military personnel, who could be relied on to remain calm, clear-thinking and responsive to orders in even the most tense of situations. But weightlessness was something new to them. Apart from its sheer novelty, it is this condition which makes life in space so different from the way we live on Earth.

Weightlessness is not a result of 'being beyond Earth's gravity', but the effect of being in 'free fall'. Stand on some bathroom scales with your arms raised; then drop your arms. For the split second your arms are falling freely — and weightless — the scales will register a lower weight. A spacecraft in orbit around the Earth is in permanent free fall, and so its equipment and occupants are permanently weightless.

Early flights showed that space travellers adjusted quickly to weightlessness, at least in the short term. Apart from minor inconveniences, which included sleeping with one's arms up, there were no problems in controlling the spacecraft. Problems which did arise involved food — both its intake and its disposal. Three-course restaurant meals were clearly out of the question, as the food would have floated off the plate, and the accompanying glass of vintage claret would have rapidly fragmented into a thousand droplets. The first space travellers ate dehydrated food cubes which they reconstituted with water, while squeezing their liquid refreshments out of tubes. As things improved, space food began to look more like the airline lunch-tray variety, capable of being warmed at the flick of a

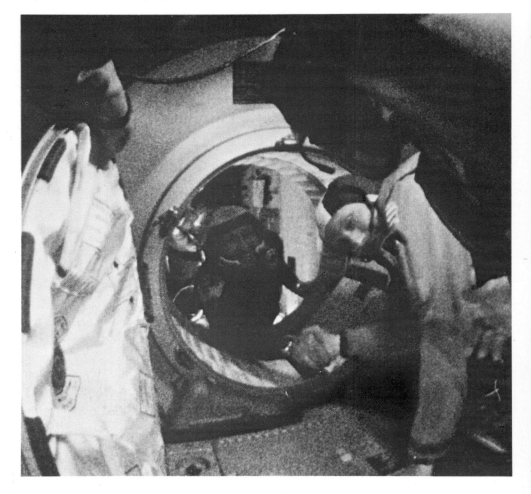

previous page A Space City of the future. In this space colony thousands of people can live and work in unpolluted conditions. The spinning cylinder generates 'gravity', power comes from huge solar panels, and external mirrors control 'daylight'. Space colonies like this may well be a reality 50 years from now.

above Detente in space: mission commanders Leonov and Stafford clasp hands across the hatch linking their docked Apollo and Soyuz craft.

right Riding piggyback atop a Jumbo jet, Space Shuttle Enterprise starts her maiden flight.

switch. On long-term missions, however, space travellers craved a choice of tastes and textures, which at last necessitated real food, appropriately packaged to be eaten in weightless conditions.

The long-term effects of weightlessness are more far-reaching than anyone had expected. Most of the Skylab crews experienced a form of space sickness, which seems unrelated to the kind of motion sickness familiar to Earth-dwellers. More serious was the crew members' muscle wastage. Despite rigorous exercise programmes designed to counteract the 'floppiness' of weightlessness, the last Skylab astronauts returned to Earth lengthened by 5 cm (nearly 2 inches), with a 2½ cm (1 inch) reduction recorded around their calves. Excessive loss of body fluid weakened them badly, and it was often a matter of several weeks before they readjusted to Earth's gravity and were able to walk properly. Some scientists see these signs as indicating that future space explorers must be born and bred in weightless conditions for that purpose alone; they may never visit Earth at all.

Worst of all, it seems that space does really get into your bones — in the nastiest way of all. Skylab astronauts registered continuous calcium loss from their bones all the time they were aloft, seriously weakening their skeletons. Although these losses were made good on returning to Earth, where calcium was again transferred normally between blood and bones, it is this effect which may determine the ultimate duration of future space voyages. Unless the cause of calcium loss is found, whether it be a result of weightlessness or of some other factor, flights are currently limited to one year only. Yet the Soviet authorities claim that their Salyut 6 crew, who spent six months in space, are healthy on account of an 'exceptionally conscientious' attitude to exercise. Whether the Russians have discovered the remedy or their claim is simply exaggerated remains to be seen.

At any rate, the emphasis — for the remainder of this century — will be on shorter flights, undertaken by people who are far more 'ordinary' than the supermen of the 1960s. The change has come about with the introduction of NASA's reusable workhorse, the Space Shuttle. There are actually four space-going shuttles in NASA's fleet, all named after ships which made historic voyages of discovery — Columbia, Challenger, Discovery and Atlantis. Enterprise, the first Shuttle, will never fly into space. It was a prototype built for early tests and it now performs valuable service at airshows publicising NASA's work. Breaking somewhat with tradition, NASA only agreed to its name after intense pressure from *Startrek* fans!

Each Shuttle looks like a delta-winged aircraft, and with a length of 37.1 metres (122 feet) and wingspan of 23.8 metres (78 feet), it is similar in size to a DC9 jetliner. However, Shuttle is, to all intents and purposes, a glider. It is launched into space by external boosters (the two solid fuel boosters are reused on subsequent missions), spends up to ten days in orbit, then — empty of any fuel, for even tiny amounts could be a fire hazard — glides back to Earth to land on a specially-constructed 4.6 km (15,000 ft)-long runway at the Kennedy Space Center. It takes only a matter of days to ready a Shuttle for its next mission.

Because Shuttle is reusable, it is cutting the cost of space missions by up to 90 per cent. This means that many of the routine uses of space — such as communications or resources surveys — have become available to many more nations who can 'buy space' for their satellites in Shuttle's cargo bay. The Shuttle releases them into orbit (with the aid of extra small boosters, if necessary), and, best of all, can retrieve damaged or malfunctioning satellites — cutting costs once again. These tasks and many others — from commercial pharmaceutical production to supervising an ant colony — keep the Shuttle crew busy throughout a

mission. Shuttle's pilots are trained astronauts with years of flying experience; but the 'mission specialists' are enthusiastic, somewhat fit scientists — both men and women — who supervise their nation's space experiments. NASA is even considering allowing VIPs from industry and 'creative writers' on the occasional flight. But they warn that potential Dan Dares will need to be fit — and undertake two months' training!

One of the Shuttle's major cargoes, apart from the Space Telescope (Chapter 2), is the European Space Agency's Spacelab space station, which sits in the cargo bay. Spacelab, and other space factories, are taking advantage of space conditions for some unique industrial experiments. The airless, weightless environment is ideal for growing perfect supersized crystals, as well as for the manufacture of new alloys and ultrapure glass; the optics, communications and electronics industries should benefit handsomely. Other tasks of these first space factories will be as diverse as medicine processing and the robot-controlled assembly of huge girders for future space stations. In every way Shuttle will make space an economic proposition.

This is not to say that our past space ventures have been a waste of money — quite the opposite. Man not only flies through space, but also uses it to his own advantage. Life today would be very different if it were not for the swarm of satellites now circling our planet, each sent up to perform its own specialist task. Some satellites, such as those designed for astronomical or geophysical research, have little effect on our daily lives. But try to imagine the modern world without communications satellites. There would be limited international telephone links, no transoceanic television broadcasts and a noticeable lack of immediacy in everything from business transactions to the lunchtime news. 'Comsats', such as those on the world-wide Intelsat network, travel in synchronous orbits, taking the same time to complete an orbit as the Earth takes to turn, so they appear to hover above the same spot on the equator, at a height of 35,800 km (22,240 miles). Television signals and telephone conversations beamed up to them are boosted electronically and beamed back down to where they are needed. The latest generation of comsats can handle over a dozen colour TV channels and some 10,000 telephone calls simultaneously, but even

their capacity will be insufficient by the early 1980s.

Other satellites touch our lives less directly but are no less important. Meteorological satellites, such as ESA's Meteosat, send back daily television pictures of Earth's weather patterns, as well as measuring temperature and cloud cover. Because all nations cooperate in exchanging weather satellite results, warnings of impending disasters — tornados and hurricanes — can often be given in time. Then there are the Landsat craft designed to map the Earth's resources, checking for diseased crops, pollution or the position of fish shoals. Navigational satellites act as precision beacons for ships and aircraft, and there is even a whole series of satellites (code-named Oscar) containing equipment designed and built by radio 'hams'.

More controversial are reconnaissance satellites, usually launched in north—south orbits to give them the capacity to scan the whole world as it spins underneath. Many of the Soviet Cosmos series are spy satellites, photographing target areas and parachuting the results to ground in film canisters. The details visible can be gauged from the claim that satellites in the American Big Bird reconnaissance series are able to distinguish military from civilian personnel on the basis of uniform! It is now maintained, on reasonably firm evidence, that both major powers are developing killer satellites, capable of blasting the other's spy satellites out of space — and probably worse.

Standing on the threshold of the third

millenium, how will Man of the immediate future try to tame space? Some see a world powered by microwave beams sent down from huge sail-shaped solar power satellites, several kilometres across and orbiting in perpetual undimmed sunshine. Space visionary and writer Arthur C. Clarke, who forecast global communication satellites back in 1945, sees trips to the Moon as commonplace by the turn of the century — and at competitive prices. If NASA finds the money, there will be bases on the Moon and preparations should be well advanced for the first manned mission to Mars. Princeton physicist Gerard O'Neill has an enthusiastic and devoted following for his alternative and practical scheme for space colonies: spinning cylinders in space able to accommodate thousands, and later millions, of people, who would live on the cylinders' inner surfaces. They would reap the benefits of permanent sunshine, lack of pollution and controlled climate — as well as helping to ease the ever-increasing world population problem.

Any further speculation on Man's future relationship with space would probably end up very wide of the mark. Already technology is far in advance of its full exploitation, and the picture in AD 2000 may turn out to be quite different, as we begin to realize these opportunities. Space is our oyster. And should anyone need reminding of this, British astronomer Sir Fred Hoyle has some typically unconventional words on the subject: 'Space isn't remote at all. It's only an hour's drive away if your car could go straight upwards'.

left *Ed White, first American to walk in space, floats outside his Gemini 4 capsule on 3 June 1965. EVAs such as this will become commonplace among Space Shuttle crews, who will need to become adept at repairing minor faults on payloads despatched into orbit by the Shuttle.*

right *Like a fish on a line, a Space Shuttle hangs above her enormous fuel tank, flanked by the two reusable solid fuel rocket boosters. After a mission, a complete Shuttle refit and maintenance only takes a few days.*

EXPLORING THE SOLAR SYSTEM

In a recent *Time* magazine article marking the tenth anniversary of Man's first lunar landing space prophet Arthur C. Clarke wrote: 'We have bequeathed the solar system to our children, not our grandchildren, and they will be duly thankful.'

The next generation will find the way ahead in space already prepared for them. By 1990 unmanned planetary probes will have explored our solar system out to its remotest reaches, amassing a total of some 30 years' constant surveillance from space. The results of this robot reconnaissance have so far been astonishing: many of our cherished ideas about the planets have been proved wrong and whole tomes have had to be written to incorporate the new findings. 'Pretty well all we thought we knew was nonsense', says Clarke of our preprobe state of knowledge.

Only the mighty Sun stands a little aloof from this revolution in information, as befits its status as our local star and controller of its family of planets. Unlike unwary Icarus, whose wax wings melted when he approached the Sun too closely, spaceprobes do not dare to venture too near. Thus, much of our knowledge about the Sun was gleaned before the dawn of the Space Age, but this has since been supplemented in a number of important ways.

That the Sun is different from its retinue of planets is immediately obvious. With a diameter of 1.4 million km (864,000 miles), it is by far the largest body in the solar system; it is made entirely of extremely hot gases; and it is more than a thousand times as massive as its whole family put together. This last factor dictated the Sun's fate from birth. Had it been less than one-twentieth of this mass, it would have lived its life as a planet, but the tremendous heat produced by the compression of all its material under its own gravitational inpull ensured that the Sun became instead a star. Its core temperature is a staggering 14 million °C — sufficient to cause hydrogen gas, the Sun's most abundant material, to fuse into helium in the reaction which provides its source of energy. Our star works like a slowly running hydrogen bomb of cosmic proportions, converting 4 million tonnes of its nuclear fuel *every second* into the light and heat with which it bathes its family. None of the planets were sufficiently massive for their centres to achieve the high temperature which would have switched on their power supplies, and consequently they remain as cold inert globes.

The Sun's surface, the photosphere, is a sea of churning gases. In places, however, the ebb and flow is interrupted by darker spots, which at 4500 °C are some 1500 °C cooler than their surroundings. Sunspots sometimes grow so large — up to hundreds of thousands of kilometres across — that we can see them from Earth when the Sun is dimmed by mist; Chinese astronomers have recorded them for many centuries past.

Sunspots come and go, and they are just one sign that our local star is not completely constant. Every eleven years or so the number of spots builds up to a peak; the most recent maximum occurred in spring 1980. With the increase in spots comes a build-up of associated activity — great gas plumes (prominences or filaments) and glowing clouds (faculae or plages) suspended above the spots in the Sun's lower atmosphere, and titanic storms (solar flares) which spew out streams of deadly charged particles into space. Astronomers believe the culprit to be the Sun's magnetic field, twisted so much by the spinning Sun that in places it bursts through the surface to wreak havoc. And although there is now an elegant theory to explain why everything should repeat itself every eleven years, it pays not to be too certain. During the latter half of the 17th century, records show that the Sun remained spotless, and it could well repeat that performance in the future.

Solar activity — for all the far-reaching effects it produces on Earth, as described below — involves only the Sun's surface layers. There is, however, a growing suspicion that its inconstancy is more than skin deep. The Sun's size varies by 100 metres or so (one ten-millionth of its diameter) as it pulses in and out, taking from a few minutes to a couple of hours to do so. But solar expert Jack Eddy claims that the Sun is actually shrinking — and that this could be partly responsible for liberating the Sun's energy. Eddy's claim rests on decades of records of the Sun's diameter. However, the latest, most accurate measurements don't back him up — which is as well for other astronomers, who would otherwise have to revise completely their ideas of how the Sun and stars work.

There are currently more serious worries concerning the Sun's basic energy source. From capturing neutrinos — elusive subatomic particles which wing straight from the Sun's core — physicist Raymond Davis reports that all is not well. The number of neutrinos caught should accurately mirror the conditions prevailing in the solar powerhouse, and Davis is detecting far fewer than

Our mighty Sun, photographed on 10 June 1973 by astronauts on a Skylab mission. Taken in extreme ultraviolet light, the picture shows not the visible face of the Sun, but the searingly hot gases of its upper atmosphere. Although the colours are false — an artefact of laboratory processing — the brightness at any point corresponds to temperature. The plume of gas at the top extends a staggering 450,000 km (280,000 miles) into space.

predicted. Is the Sun's core cooler than calculated? Has its nuclear reactor temporarily shut down? Or is it simply that the Sun's internal make-up is different from what astronomers had thought?

Any change in or on the Sun affects our totally dependent Earth. The next time there is a total solar eclipse in your part of the world look at the Sun's pearly-bright surrounding corona, as its dazzling disc is intercepted by the brief passage of our Moon. The corona is the origin of the solar wind, a perpetual stream of atomic particles which, like the Sun's radiation, rains incessantly on to the planets and goes far beyond. At sunspot maximum the wind is extremely fierce, and solar flares fan it to its greatest violence. On reaching Earth the deadly particles entangle themselves in our magnetic field, producing glorious displays of aurorae (northern and southern lights) as they plunge harmlessly downward towards the poles. But woe betide any nation launching a manned space mission in the days following a flare, for once above our protective atmosphere their astronauts would almost certainly run the risk of severe radiation sickness.

The Sun has more subtle effects upon Earth, and both astronomers and meteorologists are busy assessing their extent. Climate is one; the Sun may have had a major part to play in causing the Ice Ages. Shorter-term weather is another: records show that superb European summers, with accompanying excellent sporting performances and wine vintages, have occurred during sunspot maximum — although the reason is hard to discover at our present state of knowledge.

The Sun's interaction with Mercury must be anything but subtle, for this tiny planet, 40 per cent larger than our Moon, lies only 58 million km (36 million miles) away. Too small to retain any atmosphere, Mercury has been scoured and buffeted by the relentless forces of space from the days of its birth. The Mariner 10 spaceprobe pictures reveal a Moon-like, crater-scarred world, evidence for Mercury's long bombardment by pieces of space debris. Even now its environment is far from kind. Temperatures during its 58 day 'daytime' exceed 400 °C — hot enough to melt lead — and drop to −170 °C during the long Mercurian night. Man is most unlikely to set foot on Mercury until he has to.

Space probes have utterly dashed any hopes that jewel-like Venus may offer a warmer welcome, for this planet, although tantalizingly similar to our own in terms of size and mass, is the solar system's closest approach to Hell. Its unbroken cloud layers reflect sunlight so well that Venus looks like a hanging lantern in our twilight skies; only the Sun and the Moon appear brighter. There were early speculations that, beneath its clouds, Venus was a moist tropical paradise. Lying only 108 million km (67 million miles) from the Sun, the planet would receive more heat, but the clouds were expected to temper this. Even before

above The totally-eclipsed Sun bathes the sea off the coast of Zanzibar with its eerie light. It is easy to understand the superstitious awe with which early man regarded eclipses, and even today we feel its effect. With the coming of darkness, flowers close, birds fly home to roost, and many still watch the spectacle with fear and dread.

right Close-up of the total eclipse of 26 February 1979, photographed in Monatana, Canada. Because the overlapping of the Moon and Sun must be so precise to produce a total eclipse, only a small region of the Earth's surface can ever see this spectacle at a given time. Astronomers sometimes trek halfway across the world to the eclipse site, where they make special studies of the Sun's pearly corona — the faint outer atmosphere visible only when the Sun's bright disc is blotted out.

the coming of probes, flaws in this rosy picture began to emerge. In particular, astronomers bouncing trains of radio waves off the planet (a technique called radar astronomy) believed that they had detected a rugged, cratered and searingly hot surface. They also found that Venus was spinning on its axis very slowly — every 243 Earth days — and in the opposite direction from normal.

Early fly-by probes served only to confirm the grim picture. When the Russian Venera series of spacecraft first attempted to land, several craft were simply crushed out of existence by the enormously high atmospheric pressure before they could even reach the surface. But later Veneras were to obtain the first close-up colour photographs of Venus' flat, rock-strewn deserts. More recently, Russian and American probes have mapped the surface by radar from orbit, discovering mountains even higher than Earth's Mount Everest, and volcanoes which may still be active.

Men will be in no hurry to follow in their wake. A space-farer on Venus's surface would find himself simultaneously roasted, suffocated, squashed and corroded — by the 500 °C temperature, the choking carbon dioxide atmosphere, the enormous atmospheric pressure (90 times that on Earth) and the gentle rain of sulphuric acid from the clouds. Add to this the fine suspension of high-altitude sulphur particles, the blood-red quality of light at the surface and the presence of huge chasms — and it becomes easy to see why Venus is best left alone for the moment.

Had Earth been only a fraction nearer the Sun, it, too, would have suffered Venus's fate. The carbon dioxide making up Earth's early atmosphere dissolved in our oceans and later became locked up in deposits of rock. But Venus, only 30 per cent closer to the Sun, was always just too hot for water to exist as a liquid. Its carbon dioxide remained to trap the Sun's heat, so that Venus, because of this 'runaway greenhouse effect', is now the hottest and most hostile planet in the solar system.

In every way we have Earth's watery covering to thank for our very existence. Biologists now believe that the chemical reactions which ultimately gave rise to living cells took place much more efficiently in the warm shallow seas, and think it unlikely that waterless planets will be able to harbour life. So far, Earth is the only planet we know with large quantities of liquid water.

At 12,760 km (7,927 miles) across, Earth is the largest and most massive of the inner planets, and in two ways this has helped to encourage the flowering of life. First, compression by the weight of overlying layers has made Earth's interior hot, which has resulted in warm currents of partially molten rock which rise to the surface layers and propel the light rocks forming the continents around the globe. Continental drift (the result of a process called plate tectonics) must have made it easier for life to evolve in both form and variety as its environment constantly changed. The process continues today, and we see the evidence in the form of earthquakes and volcanoes. Second, the Earth's large mass

left *Next-door neighbour Venus, photographed in 1974 by the Mariner 10 spaceprobe, is the nearest world to Earth. She hides her secrets under a dense, unbroken mantle of cloud, whose striking convection patterns are revealed in this false-colour picture.*

right *Mercury, photographed by the same probe, is revealed as having a rough, cratered surface uncannily like the Moon's. As well as showing the scars of intense meteoroid bombardment in the past, Mercury still suffers even today; as the closest planet to the Sun, it is blasted by the solar wind and showered with deadly particles during solar flares.*

below *The slender crescents of the Earth and its Moon hang isolated in space. This beautiful photograph — the first ever taken of the Earth-Moon system — is a last backward glance by the Voyager 1 spacecraft as it sped away on its mission to Jupiter and beyond, never to return home.*

enabled our planet to retain an adequate atmosphere, affording fragile life some protection from the ravages of space. It absorbs the most harmful of the Sun's rays and acts as a shield against meteoroid bombardment, although the largest bodies have always been able to reach ground and some have excavated spectacular craters.

Our small, airless companion world, the Moon, was born with none of these advantages, and its pitted blackened surface testifies to billions of years' bombardment from space. The very worst scars are easily visible from the 385,000 km (238,000 miles) distant Earth as the 'face' of the 'Man in the Moon'. These colossal basins, mistaken for seas by the early telescopic observers, are a legacy of impacts by huge meteoroids, each over 100 km (60 miles) across, which later filled up with dark upwelling magma.

The Apollo results tell of a long-dead, shattered world, baked by the unrelenting Sun to over 110 °C during the 14 day lunar 'daytime' and chilled to —155 °C at night. The side of the Moon we do not see from Earth, because our world's strong gravity

has braked the Moon's rotation, is even more rugged.

Why, then, go to the Moon? Partly for the same reasons we go into space: to utilize the black skies, the vacuum conditions, and the low gravity. Partly because Apollo has found its soil to be far richer in valuable minerals such as calcium, aluminium and titanium than Earth's, all there for the taking. And last, the Moon will give us practice in living on other worlds. It is our first stepping-stone into space.

Man's second stepping-stone will undoubtedly be Mars. At 6,787 km (4,217 miles) across, it is only just over half Earth's size, and it circles the Sun at a chilly 227.9 million km (142 million miles); of all the planets, however, it is the most Earth-like. Through their telescopes earlier astronomers saw a ruddy world with white polar caps and green markings which, like vegetation, changed in shape with the seasons. Some fancied that they could see faint dark lines linking the poles with the patches — were these canals built by intelligent Martians to irrigate their deserts? At 24 hours

37 minutes, even the rotation period of Mars resembles ours.

However, the first fly-by probes, Mariners 4, 6 and 7, discovered a depressingly Moon-like, cratered planet with an atmosphere of carbon dioxide ten times thinner than expected. The canals were optical illusions; the green markings just darker zones of rock periodically covered and uncovered by seasonal dust storms.

Then Mariner 9, sent into Mars orbit in 1971, revealed a much more interesting world. It mapped the unknown northern hemisphere, discovering huge volcanoes up to 29 km (18 miles) high and 515 km (320 miles) across, and finding colossal canyons 5,000 km (3,000 miles) long. Both features would easily dwarf their counterparts on Earth. There was water locked up in the polar caps and — most exciting of all — what looked like dried-up river beds. Water means life, and this is the reason why the two Viking lander craft which touched down on Mars in 1976 carried a battery of experiments to test the soil for simple life forms.

There was an initial flurry of intense excitement when the first apparently positive results were transmitted. Later, however, scientists realized that the rapid reactions were chemical rather than biological, and they have now reluctantly concluded that Mars, at least in the bleak deserts where the Vikings landed, does not support life. As long as there are 'ifs' and 'possiblys', the search for life will go on, and the Martian landers of the future will carry special equipment to sniff out life. Mars's water may be locked up in a permafrost layer in its soil — like the Earth's tundra regions — and 'if' the climate were to warm up, the water might flow again. Conditions in Mars's sheltered valleys are more benign than the —120 °C to +25 °C temperature range of the equatorial deserts, 'possibly' allowing primitive life to get a hold. But on the basis of our present evidence, it seems that Man will be the first living organism to walk on the Martian sands.

Despite their many differences there is

still an overall similarity between all the inner or 'terrestrial' planets. They have solid surfaces with mountains, valleys and craters; their atmospheres are shallow and generally thin; and all are comfortably small in size. This reassuring familiarity vanishes once we cross the asteroid belt. We enter the zone of the gas giants — Jupiter, Saturn, Uranus and Neptune.

Greatest of all is Jupiter, more than twice as massive as all the other planets combined and a thousand times larger in volume than Earth. Most of this vast bulk is gas, mainly hydrogen, helium, methane and ammonia. But Jupiter probably has a small rocky or metallic core, which because of the planet's great mass is very hot, and Jupiter actually radiates twice as much heat as it receives from the distant Sun. However, its cloud tops are at a frigid −150 °C, and there is no danger of Jupiter suddenly turning into a star — it would need to be some 50 times more massive for that transformation to occur.

In a telescope the planet looks rather like a yellow and brown striped humbug, with the 4 brightest of its 16 moons strung out in a line alongside it. The stripes are actually convection currents in Jupiter's turbulent atmosphere — pale areas ascending, dark areas descending — drawn out into belts by the planet's incredibly rapid rotation. Jupiter's 'day' is over in less than ten hours. As a result, it is fascinating to watch the rapidly changing appearance of this planet in even a small telescope: belts and markings can be tracked across its disc; sudden spots and whorls break out as atmospheric currents collide; and the moons pass behind and in front of the planet, casting their shadows across Jupiter's frozen cloud tops.

One spot has persisted in Jupiter's atmosphere for at least 100 years, and some records suggest as much as 300 years. The Great Red Spot, which floats around the planet just south of its equator, is a gigantic oval which could contain some twelve Earths. The Voyager spaceprobes discovered and filmed hundreds more spots whose structure changed by the minute, but most were colourless and not nearly as spectacular and long-lasting as their prototype. Voyager meteorologists have compared the spots to anticyclones (high-pressure regions) in Earth's atmosphere, and they tentatively ascribe the Great Red Spot's colour to as yet unidentified substances dragged up from deep in Jupiter's atmosphere which redden on exposure to sunlight.

As well as feeling that they are getting to grips with the composition of the giant planet's atmosphere, Voyager scientists have found a great deal more to get excited

The Blue Planet: our own world, photographed from space. At the centre lurks the dramatic vortex of Hurricane Gladys (1968), in which winds of up to 150 km/h (95 mph) swirl around the still, central 'eye'.

about. Jupiter's skies, they find, are racked by staggeringly brilliant lightning flashes. At night they sparkle with aurorae, caused by electrically charged particles trapped in the planet's enormously powerful magnetic field, which would dazzle us on Earth. And the Voyagers find Jupiter to be encircled by very faint thin rings, which lie surprisingly close to the planet itself.

Among the Voyagers' many scoops were their close-up surveys of Jupiter's major moons, Io, Europa, Ganymede and Callisto, each comparable in size with the planet Mercury — some even larger. Callisto, composed of equal amounts of rock and ice, is the solar system's most cratered body, and possibly the least

altered of them all. Ganymede has puzzling signs that plate tectonics has been at work. Europa, smooth and flat, looks like a 19th century drawing of Mars, complete with straight canals. Io is the *enfant terrible* of the Sun's family: with eight active volcanoes, at least a hundred extinct cones, a constantly changing patchwork surface and a trailing cloud of sulphur, it is an enigma.

After the spectacular discoveries made in the Jupiter system, scientists were prepared when Voyager 1, and then Voyager 2, flew past Saturn in the early 1980s. What staggered them was the tremendously enthusiastic public reaction to the photographs. Saturn, with its glorious rings, is evidently everyone's idea

of a pin-up planet.

Pre-Voyager, Saturn was known as *the* planet with *the* rings — a smaller, less squally version of Jupiter, surrounded by three broad, thin rings and ten satellites. The first surprise came as Voyager 1 approached the rings — from below. Against the sunlight, Voyager's TV cameras picked out thousands of fine divisions in the rings. When all the pictures were returned, scientists realised that Saturn has not just three wide rings, but thousands upon thousands of narrow ringlets — each ringlet made up of billions of chunks of ice and rock. Nor are all the ringlets circular. Some are elliptical; others are discontinuous curves. The

right *The biggest volcano yet discovered: Olympus Mons on Mars. This colossus towers 26 km (16 miles) above the plains, and measures 600 km (375 miles) across. The boundary which rings the volcano is a sheer cliff some 4 km (2½ miles) high, and even the central crater is 70 km (45 miles) in diameter. Although now inactive, the extensive lava flows testify to many enormous eruptions in the past.*

below *Sunset over the sands of Mars, as seen from the Viking 1 lander. Viking's camera scanned from the left as the Sun sank towards the horizon, taking ten minutes to cover the 120° wide view.*

far right *Jupiter photographed from a distance of 28.5 million km (18 million miles) by the Voyager 1 spaceprobe. The Great Red Spot, circled by scudding cloud systems, is at top right. Above the heaving atmosphere float two of the planet's peculiar moons (centre left and far left). Since this picture was taken, the Voyager 2 probe has discovered another moon of Jupiter, bringing the total to 14; yet another is suspected.*

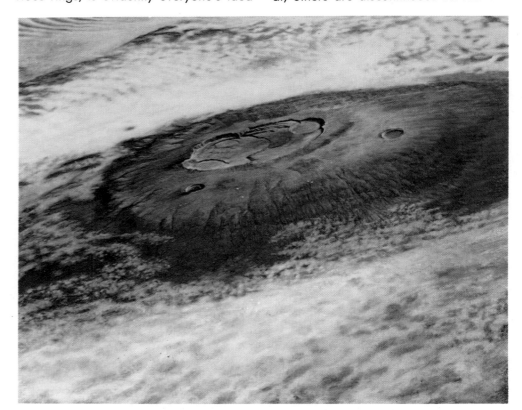

most peculiar ring of all was discovered by Voyager 1 well outside the body of the main rings. This 'F-ring' consists of two ringlets actually plaited together. Astronomers now think the F-ring's peculiar appearance is caused by the gravity of a pair of newly-discovered 'shepherd' satellites lying to either side.

Thanks to the Voyagers, Saturn's grand total of satellites stands at 23. Many are little more than icebergs, measuring only 10 km (6 miles) across. At the other end of the range is the enormous Titan, with its dense orange nitrogen atmosphere cloaking a surface which may be covered in oceans of liquid methane. As for Saturn itself, it

hides its features under a haze; but the computer-processed Voyager images reveal its storms, together with winds that blow at 1,800 km per hour (1,100 mph).

Beyond Saturn roll two more gas giants, both unknown to the ancients. Uranus, some four times the size of Earth, was found by William Herschel in 1781, and is just visible without a telescope if you know where to look. It has a faint set of rings, discovered by accident in 1977, which are a certain lure for Voyager 2 when it arrives in 1986. Astronomers hope that even more remote Neptune, virtually Uranus's twin, will be visited by the same spacecraft in 1989. They have already bet odds-on that it will turn out to have rings.

The solar system's current planetary frontier post is generally manned by strange little Pluto, which orbits the Sun every 248 years at a mean distance of 5,900 million km (3,666 million miles). Between 1979 and 1999, Pluto's eccentric path brings it closer to the Sun than Neptune, temporarily losing it this distinction — and arousing suspicion that the tiny planet, probably only 2,400 km (1,500 miles) across, is just Neptune's escaped satellite. Whatever the case, Pluto — itself discovered as late as 1930 — appears to have a moon of its own (named Charon), detected only recently on photographic plates stretching back over the decades. It is comforting to know that even though this little world is off the

Voyagers' itinerary, it is not lonely in space.

The gravitational maw of the Sun extends far beyond Pluto, perhaps halfway to the nearest star, controlling multitudes of small bodies too insignificant to have a name. Most are just loose agglomerations of ice and rock which float through space like thistledown until they are perturbed by the gravity of a passing star. Then they can be dragged down towards the Sun, getting ever hotter in their headlong flight until their ice melts, evaporates and, blown by the solar wind, streams out behind in a glorious tail. In this way a comet is born.

Many comets round the Sun and head back into the solar system's remotest reaches, freezing as they go. These may never return for millions of years. Some, however, are trapped among the planets, passing Earth regularly, and become familiar to astronomers, who name them after their discoverers. Although Edmund Halley did not, strictly speaking, discover the comet which bears his name but instead recognized a 76 year repetition in certain celestial apparitions, his comet has become the best-known. Its return in 1986 will be celebrated by 4 attempted space probe interceptions which, it is hoped, will reveal how the comet is made and which materials lurk at the solar system's furthest outposts.

After repeated circuits of the Sun the fragile comets become worn down and end their lives as clouds of dust grains. Several times a year the Earth intercepts these clouds, and we are treated to a shower of meteors or 'shooting stars' as the grains plough into our atmosphere and are consumed by friction.

Brilliant meteors (fireballs) and meteorites (which survive to hit the ground) have a different origin. They are debris from the asteroid belt — a zone containing thousands of rocky and metallic fragments up to 1,000 km (620 miles) in diameter, between the orbits of Mars and Jupiter. The recent discovery of a 300 km (190 miles) 'miniplanet' called Chiron, circling the Sun between Saturn and Uranus, suggests that there may be a second asteroid zone somewhere out there.

All scientists agree that asteroids and meteorites are of great importance to Man. Asteroids are probably the unaltered fragments of a planet which failed to be built when the solar system formed, and so by studying the make-up of meteorites we can obtain a good idea of conditions in our part of the solar system some 4,600 million years ago. Asteroids have more practical advantages for man, too. They are rich in raw materials such as iron, and with their vast numbers and virtually zero-gravity conditions they are tempting targets as the mines of the future. More romantic visionaries see them as ready-made space clippers, just waiting to have solar-powered sails attached.

For the next few centuries we will be flexing our space muscles in the solar system. It is destined to become our test strip, our laboratory and our playground. There will, of course, be those who complain about the cost of such endeavours, but they should be reminded that such carping is nothing new. When a critic protested about the financial drain imposed by Columbus's epic voyage of discovery, he was tactfully silenced by one of Queen Isabella's aides, who pointed out that the expedition had cost only about the same as a royal banquet!

top *Saturn photographed with the 1.5 metre (60 inch) reflector at the Hale Observatories. The beautiful rings — no longer a unique feature in the solar system — are made of millions of tiny chunks of rock and ice which reflect sunlight.*

above *The 30 cm (12 inch) Northumberland refractor at Cambridge was one of the telescopes used in the search for Neptune in the mid-19th century. The planet was eventually found in its predicted position by Galle at Berlin Observatory.*

right *Named after its discoverer Richard West, Comet West 1976 hangs in the twilight sky displaying its beautiful fan-like tail composed of incandescent gases. Weeks after this shot was taken, its head dramatically split into four.*

THE STARRY SKIES

For disciplines which are among the keenest users of modern technology, astronomy and space science sometimes seem to have a peculiarly anachronistic ring to them. The jargon of all scientists is laced with such newly coined words as 'quark', 'flip-flop' and 'megabyte'; yet astronomers still talk of 'alpha Ursae Minoris' (alpha of the little bear) when referring to the Pole Star, or tell colleagues that their satellite will be trained on sources towards the galactic centre 'in Sagittarius' — in the constellation of the archer.

Contemporary astronomers inherit this strange state of affairs from their forefathers. Struggling to make sense of their star-spangled skies, the ancient observers joined star to star with imaginary lines like points in a dot-to-dot puzzle book, and the shapes they invented — the constellation patterns — were handed down to posterity. Wheeling above our heads, we have a swan, a goat, an arrow, a shield, a dolphin and an eagle — and these in just one small part of the sky. With a few exceptions, the constellations bear little resemblance to their namesakes, but they are nonetheless beautiful, and useful even now. Today's astronomers use the names to divide the sky into approximately regular regions, so that every object in it can be designated a very rough location.

Names themselves can be a problem to the novice astronomer. Because of their past heritage, constellation names are in Latin, and so the patterns above become: Cygnus, Capricornus, Sagitta, Scutum, Delphinus and Aquila. Add to this the fact that star names (at least those of the brightest stars) originated with the Arabs in AD 800 — 1200, and the fun really does start! Rasalgethi, Albireo, Arcturus, Zubenelgenubi and the famous Betelgeuse (often pronounced 'beetle-juice') all have places in our skies.

Not surprisingly, the Greeks also left their mark on the starry heavens. This they did in characteristically scientific fashion by ordering the stars into different brightness classes, or 'magnitudes'. Brightest stars were assigned magnitude 1; the faintest visible were magnitude 6. When the system was slightly overhauled in the 19th century, extra magnitudes were introduced to accommodate the very brightest and faintest objects, and so the Sun ranks as *minus* 26.5, while the faintest stars which the Space Telescope can record will be magnitude *plus* 29 — the difference of 55.5 magnitudes covering a brightness range of over 10,000 million million million times.

Commemorating the Greek love of order, Johann Bayer renamed the stars in every constellation according to their brightness by assigning to each a letter of the Greek alphabet; the brightest became

above *Night falls over the Arizona Desert. As the last glow of twilight silhouettes the barren rocks, multitudes of stars start to appear in the darkening sky, until the heavens are ablaze from horizon to horizon.*

right *Star trails reveal our spinning Earth, while the huge dome of the Anglo-Australian telescope bears silent witness below. By keeping the camera shutter open for several hours, the photographer was able to record the continual wheeling of the heavens as we rotate underneath.*

alpha (followed by its constellation name), the second beta, then gamma, and so on. Four hundred years on, astronomers still use this system for naming stars, resorting to numbers when the 24 letters of the Greek alphabet run out. Thus, the brightest star in the constellation of the lyre is Vega or alpha Lyrae (alpha of the lyre); the second brightest in Leo the lion is Denebola, beta Leonis. The system sounds complicated, but it is surprisingly simple in use.

For all this meticulous classification, until the last century the stars might just as well have been fairy lights hung on strings — without a knowledge of a star's distance from Earth, none of the precise measures of position and brightness can be converted into reality, and they are of little value. In 1838, however, Friedrich Bessel succeeded in finding the distance to a star called 61 Cygni, and at last the twinkling points of light started to become real bodies.

Bessel used the 'parallax' method which many had unsuccessfully tried before, but was careful to attempt it on a nearby star in order to get it to work. He knew 61 Cygni was close — close enough to reveal its minute true movement, or 'proper motion', across the sky as it travelled through space. By carefully measuring the tiny 'jump' in the position of 61 Cygni against distant background stars when viewed from opposite sides of Earth's orbit, at six-month intervals, Bessel was able to calculate the star's distance by simple trigonometry. The result was in excess of 100 million million km (60 million million miles).

Such numbers are daunting to cope with, and astronomers dealing with distances have had to abandon miles and kilometres. Instead, they use the 'light year' — the staggering distance of 9½ million million km (6 million million miles) covered by a beam of light travelling at 300,000 km (186,000 miles) per *second*, over a period of a year. On this reckoning, 61 Cygni is a reassuring 11 light years away and Alpha Centauri, the nearest star, a mere 4½ light years distant.

Most stars do not lie anything like as close. Not only is this unnerving, but also it makes distance measurement difficult, for the parallax method cannot be used when stars are much more than 100 light years away. The astronomer must next resort to such cunning ploys as tracking the distance-revealing jostling of stars in a star cluster, and then proceed stepwise from there to build up a ladder-like scale of distances in the Universe.

By placing a thin prism ('objective prism') over the front lens of a telescope, astronomers can record the spectra of many stars simultaneously. Each star's light is dispersed into a rainbow band which is crossed by dark vertical 'absorption lines' that arise in the star's outer gas layers. A careful examination of this picture will reveal slight variations between all these spectra: to the skilled eye, they indicate differences in composition and temperature.

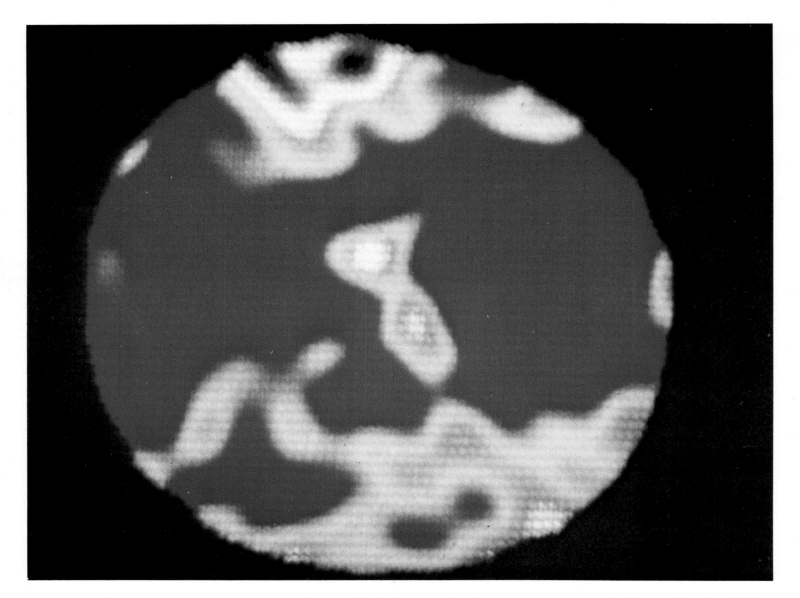

Measuring distance is only part of the battle, and two more 19th century developments had to happen before the stars could assume reality. With the double-edged sword of photography and spectroscopy astronomers were at last able to cleave deep into the mysteries of the stars, discovering the enormous range of sizes, masses, brightnesses and temperatures which exists among them.

On a velvety black transparent night the stars themselves reveal a few of their long-kept secrets. Take a star's colour, for instance: this is a rough and ready guide to its temperature. Just as a piece of metal glows red when first heated and then, as the temperature increases, ranges through amber, yellow, white and finally blue-white, so stars with different temperatures show different colours. The coolest, reddest stars are easiest to pick out — look for Antares, Betelgeuse and Aldebaran, whose temperatures are all around 3,000 ºC. Amber Arcturus is at 4,000 ºC. Then there are yellow stars such as the Sun, Canopus and Capella, whose surfaces are at 6,000 ºC. At 10,000 ºC Sirius shines diamond-white, while blue-white Rigel is close to a searing 20,000 ºC.

Without a knowledge of its distance from Earth, a star's apparent brightness is no guide to its true luminosity. Altair and Deneb, two of the three stars in the 'Summer Triangle', look about the same brightness. Yet nearby Altair is only ten times brighter than the Sun, while Deneb, 1,500 light years away, outshines our star 50,000 times. The vast majority of stars are similar to the Sun, but there is a tremendous range — from dim glowworms only a ten-thousandth as bright to glaring searchlights with 100,000 times the Sun's luminosity.

In the same way, stars range widely in their size. The tiniest stars could be hidden in one of Earth's cities; the largest are thousands of times larger than the Sun. Some of the latter prove the exception to the oft-repeated statement that 'all stars appear as points of light, even in the world's largest telescopes'. A new technique called 'speckle interferometry' reveals the discs of nearby giant stars, complete with star spots.

Many stars, such as those in the beautiful Pleiades (the Seven Sisters) live in large groups or clusters, and despite our Sun's solitary example, togetherness is the general rule. More than half the stars in the sky are actually double or even multiple, comprising two or more stars circling closely around one another. The nearest star, Alpha Centauri, is in fact a trio; Mizar in the Plough is circled by its easily seen companion Alcor; and Gemini's Castor consists of no fewer than six stars. Double stars (binaries) are both beautiful and useful; the components can be 'weighed' by close examination of their orbits, and this is the only direct means astronomers have of determining the masses of stars. The range is surprisingly narrow — most stars lie between one-tenth and ten times the Sun's mass, although there is at least one heavy-weight a hundred times heavier.

Then there are stars which break the rules. Variable stars swell and shrink, changing in size and brightness on time-scales ranging from hours to years. Pulsars spin dozens of times every second, flashing out rays like a lighthouse beam. Novae greedily suck material off their companions and suffer cosmic convulsions for their misdemeanours. Supernovae are stars which blow themselves entirely to bits.

Despite the enormous range we find among the stars, our Sun falls reassuringly in the middle on every count. It is a completely normal, average star. But how can astronomers make sense of the stars in the face of all this variety? Are there any common threads?

The answer is a resounding 'yes', for all the years of cataloguing and classifying have now paid off and no longer do astronomers merely catch stars as specimens in celestial butterfly nets. The variety among stars tells a story: the story of a star's life.

left   The face of a giant star, obtained by combining 20 photographs made with the speckle interferometer shown on the right. Betelgeuse, with a diameter of some 550 million km (345 million miles) is one of the biggest stars known, but appears only as a bright point of light, even in the world's largest telescope, unless the speckle technique is used. Dark regions on the disc are 'starspots' — cooler zones like sunspots, but hundreds of times larger.

right   Astronomer Roger Lynds, lying in the observing cage of Kitt Peaks's Mayall 4 metre (155 inch) telescope, adjusts the speckle interferometer camera which he helped to design. By taking very fast photographs which 'freeze' the twinkling of stars caused by our shifting atmosphere, astronomers have been able to discern extremely fine details — such as nearby star discs or close double stars — which are unobservable by conventional techniques.

below   Togetherness in space: the twin star clusters of h and chi Persei, both dimly visible as hazy patches in the sky, and seen to perfection in a pair of binoculars. The stars making up these clusters are extremely young, and have not yet had enough time to move far away from their birthplaces.

ASHES TO ASHES

The year 1781 found French astronomer Charles Messier putting the finishing touches to a list of deceptive fuzzy objects which had sidetracked him in his obsessive search for comets. One object so dismissed was a troublesomely bright patch just below the stars which form Orion's 'belt'. This 'Orion Nebula' is easily more important than a million comets. It is part of a huge gas cloud — just one of hundreds surrounding us in space — in which stars are beginning to form. In the nebula itself some have just been born, and their new fires are exciting the swirling gas to glow.

The story of a star starts here, as it must have done for our Sun and its family nearly 5,000 million years ago. A large cold cloud of gas and tiny dust grains — soot from the surfaces of cool stars — is given a squeeze. This compression, which may be generated by the shock waves from a nearby supernova or by the gas cloud simply slowing down in its journey through space, forces it to collapse. Gravity takes over and the cloud contracts ever more quickly, breaking into fragments as it does so. But now each rounded fragment collapses independently under its own gravity. It becomes hotter towards its centre as the compression increases, and spins faster as its earlier slow rotation is intensified by the shrinkage. The fragment is now a 'protostar' surrounded by a cocoon of dust, and although invisible, heat radiation discloses its presence to infrared astronomers.

As this collapse continues, the ever-increasing spin flattens the fragment into a disc shape and the heavy dust grains start to settle thickly into the plane of the disc. While the gas still draws itself in, the grains jostle together and stick, drawing more of their fellows to themselves as their gravity steadily increases. The gas is now extremely hot and dense at the centre of the fragment, but the outer grain bundles — now 'protoplanets' of roughly spherical shape, each some thousands of kilometres across — can grab hold of some of the cooler, slower-moving gas out there. These young planets, like the outer worlds of our solar system, develop huge deep atmospheres as a result, but their companion worlds closer to the protostar cannot hope to snatch at the hot rapidly swirling gas there, and remain small.

In the middle of its young family the protostar is reaching a crucial stage. Its central temperature has now risen to over a million °C and seems poised to increase inexorably as collapse goes on. However, when it reaches about 10 million °C, a sudden change occurs. The gas at the core is now so hot and dense that nuclear fusion is suddenly forced upon it. The reaction produces an enormous flood of energy,

which surges through the protostar and holds it up against further contraction. For a while, at least, the massive nuclear forces win the day against gravity. At this point a star is born.

Young stars are easy to spot in the night sky. They live in groups of a few hundred called 'open clusters', each member a tiny fragment of its original gas cloud. Some, like the stars in the Orion Nebula, are so young that their gas cloud still wreathes them. In the slightly older Pleiades cluster each star is cocooned in a faint haze of dust grains which will eventually be dispersed by stellar winds. Age is, of course, relative: the infant Pleiades are some 60 million years old.

Once a star has been born, it changes very little in outward appearance. After an extremely brief period of 'growing up', during which it blows away surrounding cobwebs of dust, it settles down to a period of sedate middle-age lasting for some 90 per cent of its life span. Even though nearly all stars shine by the same process — producing energy by hydrogen-to-helium fusion in their cores — by no means do they live for the same length of time. As in the case of human beings, a star's life expectancy depends on its mass.

Although astronomers are hard-pressed to explain why stars should have different birth-weights, they know that mass makes a tremendous difference to the reaction rates inside a star. Stars much heavier than the Sun rip through their fuel at a profligate tempo, shining a fierce blue-white as their nuclear fires are stoked up. They may only survive for a few million years and then die as spectacularly as they lived. Stars like the Sun, on the other hand, are only moderate consumers; they shine a placid yellow and have lifetimes running into thousands of millions of years. At the far end of the scale there are true celestial misers, dim red dwarf stars only a tenth of the Sun's mass which have been eking out their slender resources since the Universe began some 15,000 million years ago.

There comes a time in every star's life, however, when it runs out of fuel. Whether it dies with a bang or with a whimper once again depends on its mass. Sun-sized stars — and this description covers most — feel the end approaching after a respectable lifetime of some 10,000 million years, when they have converted all the hydrogen in their cores to helium. Their outward energy

Visible to the unaided eye as a hazy patch marking Orion's sword, the Orion Nebula is just a tiny part of a vast gas cloud which is in the process of collapsing and fragmenting to form stars. New stars have already come into being in this region, and their energetic ultraviolet radiation excites the surrounding gas to glow with a ghostly radiance.

left This celestial chess-piece — actually the Horsehead Nebula in Orion — is not a hole in space, but obscuration produced by large quantities of interstellar dust. These tiny dust grains, believed to have evaporated from the surfaces of cool stars, may ultimately combine to make planetary systems around young, forming stars.

below While making a thorough survey of the uncharted Southern Hemisphere skies, the UK Schmidt telescope in Australia took time off to take some spectacular photographs (such as that of eta Carinae, right). Schmidt telescopes have wide, undistorted fields of view and are ideal for taking pictures of large nearby gas clouds.

right The eta Carinae nebula, enigma of the southern heavens. The glowing gas is excited by many young stars, notably eta Carinae itself, one of the most massive and luminous stars known. This star has faded in just a century from being the second brightest in the sky to borderline naked-eye visibility today.

overleaf Clouds of dusty gas cocoon the young stars making up the Pleiades (or Seven Sisters) star cluster. As these stars mature they will cast off their dusty mantles into space.

flow dwindles fast and gravity is quick to reassert itself. The dead helium core collapses under the pull and heats up so rapidly that it causes a surrounding narrow shell of hydrogen higher up in the star suddenly to switch on fusion reactions. The effect is instantaneous: with the higher site of nuclear burning, the outer layers of the star balloon out. Its gases cool dramatically as they expand. The star has become a red giant. Swelling to hundreds of times its former size, the star may engulf some of its family of planets. Earth could well suffer this fate, but long before it happens, life will have been rendered impossible by the heat of the Sun's steadily advancing surface.

For all its impressiveness, a red giant, such as Betelgeuse or Antares, is a flimsy thing. Gas leaks away continuously from the surface, where the low gravity offers little restraint. Bereft of this control, the red giant pulsates, changing irregularly in size and brightness over periods of about a year — until it all becomes too much for the old star. Very gently, and for reasons which are by no means completely understood, its outer layers lift off into space, forming an expanding cosmic 'smoke ring' around the now-exposed stellar core. This surrounding 'planetary nebula', so-called because it can look like the disc of a planet in a small telescope, is a temporary, but very beautiful, phase in a star's death throes.

When the nebula has dispersed, all that remains is the dense, collapsed core. It is a bizarre relic: an object with most of the star's mass, shrunken into a body about the size of a small planet. White dwarf stars like this are still technically made of gas, but it is packed so densely that a spoonful would weigh about a tonne! Gas in this state is said to be 'degenerate', which partly helps to explain a recent learned paper entitled 'Recent developments in the theory of degenerate dwarfs'!

White dwarfs have no remaining energy reserves, and shine only because they are slowly leaking away their heat into space.

Although their numbers must run into millions, only the nearest and brightest can be seen at all, and one of these is the companion to Sirius, the Dog Star, appropriately nicknamed 'the Pup'.

Growing older, white dwarfs become cooler, redder and fainter still, until the very last glimmer dies away. All that remains is a cold dark globe, forlornly circled by its long-bereft planet family.

Death for the massive, spendthrift star is a far less delicate affair. A star more than about five times heavier than the Sun, having used up its fuel in record time, will also find itself in the same position as lesser stars, with gravity poised to win. Massive

stars have vast gravitational reserves which, to begin with, take over and crush the dead core even more viciously. At this stage the story differs. Contraction makes the central temperature rise to an alarming 100 million °C. Suddenly the 'dead' core springs to life, as the helium nuclei fuse together to make carbon, and the star acquires a completely new energy source to keep it shining.

Just as leopards cannot change their spots, so huge stars cannot alter their rate of fuel consumption and soon they are back to square one, this time with a core of inert carbon being crushed under gravity. However, if they are massive enough, their

central temperature can even rise high enough to ignite carbon, and these nuclei then fuse to make heavier elements such as silicon and magnesium. In this way a massive star can keep going, changing uncertainly in size and surface temperature as it undergoes internal traumas. Finally, it is left with a core of iron. Once again it tries the trick of core collapse — but this time with disastrous results. The central temperature reaches a thousand million °C, sufficient to ignite iron; but instead of giving out energy, iron fusion reactions need to take it in. Desperate to keep going, the star turns to its only available source of energy to power this rogue reaction, and allows gravity to

shrink its core still further. The rise in temperature hurls the nuclei together so violently that they are smashed into a surging torrent of particles which rages through the star. It disintegrates catastrophically in a supernova explosion, glaring brighter than ten thousand million Suns on its funeral pyre — a fitting end for so mighty a star. But sometimes it is not the end.

As is often the case in astronomy, the evidence for this came about rather unexpectedly. Late in 1967, research student Jocelyn Bell (now Dr Burnell) was making the first observations with a newly designed

left *The awesome fury of a nuclear explosion is the equivalent of just a tiny fraction of the energy which powers a star. Starlight is fuelled by reactions like this occurring deep inside a star.*

below *Stardeath! The Helix nebula represents the quiet demise of a star of the Sun's mass, in which a former red giant has gently puffed away its outer layers, revealing its white-hot core (centre). This white dwarf star will gradually cool to a black ember.*

radio telescope at Cambridge when she picked up a pulsing signal. It repeated with such uncanny regularity — every 1.3373 seconds — that it became unofficially dubbed LGM 1 (for Little Green Men 1), following some none-too-serious suggestions that the signal was a message broadcast by an extraterrestrial civilization.

The radio astronomers, headed by Tony Hewish, sought a natural cause, and came up with one that sounded almost as farfetched. The culprit, they suggested, was an ultradense star only 20 km (12 miles) across, which whips around on its axis every 1.3373 seconds shooting out beams of radiation from its poles. Like a sweeping lighthouse lamp, the object only registers when its beam flashes across Earth.

As if one freak star were not enough, CP1919 (LGM 1's official designation) was rapidly joined by dozens of other 'pulsars', all demanding an explanation for their origin. The clue came when a pulsar spinning at the incredibly rapid rate of 30 times a second turned up in the Crab Nebula — the gaseous wreck of a star which went supernova in AD 1054. Here was the answer. Pulsars are the ultracrushed cores of stars which have exploded.

These weird stellar corpses come into being when a supernova leaves behind a core of about twice the Sun's mass. Gravity is too strong even to let the core bow out as a white dwarf, and continues squeezing until its particles have merged to form neutrons and its diameter has shrunk to a few kilometres. The resulting neutron star spins rapidly at first, but beaming away its energy as a pulsar slows it down, and after a million years or so the pulses stop.

Astronomers know of some 300 pulsars, and so space must harbour thousands more neutron stars. Like planets, they are solid, but there the resemblance ends. A pinhead of their material would weigh a million tonnes, and their surface gravity is so enormous that an assault on one of their millimetre-high mountains would require more energy than a man could exert over his entire lifetime.

Gravity is the undisputed winner in the story of a star, and it holds the ultimate trump card too. This it brings into play if a supernova has the temerity to leave behind a core weighing more than three solar masses. Now collapse proceeds inexorably, for no material, not even neutrons, can resist so mighty a pull. As the core shrinks, the surface gravity soars and the escape velocity increases until it reaches the

This sequence of pictures, taken over the course of a year, shows stardeath at its most extreme. From beginnings not even visible in the top exposure a supernova explodes (arrowed) to become almost as bright as its parent galaxy of 100,000 million stars. This blaze of glory is only transitory, however, for only months later it has faded drastically and will ultimately burn up completely, never to pierce the heavens with its light again.

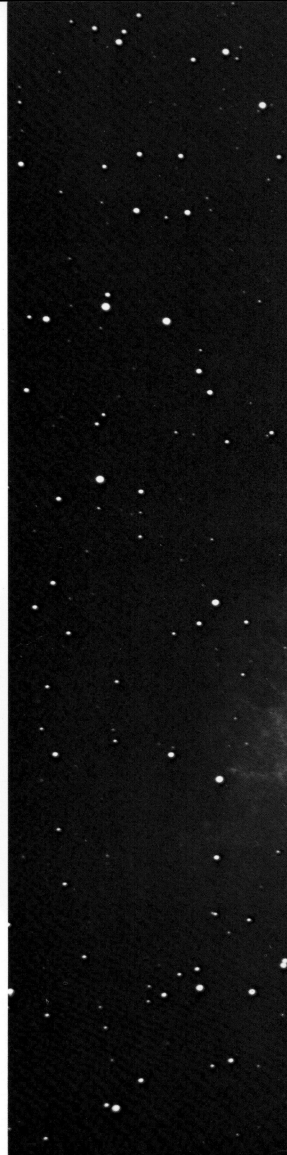

speed limit of the Universe — the velocity of light. At this point the object becomes a black hole.

But gravity does not stop there. Inside the 'event horizon' — the spherical surface a few km across where the escape velocity equals that of light — collapse continues. As no light or information can ever reach us from inside, we are literally in the dark as to what happens within the event horizon, but mathematicians calculate that the core has no choice but to be crushed to an infinitely small point. This gory fate would also overtake any space traveller unwary enough to fall into the black hole, a point much-beloved of science fiction writers. But do we really run this risk once we start to travel to the stars? 'Unlikely', scoffs a distinguished astronomer, pointing out that the chances of a spacecrew meeting up with a black hole are considerably less than those of hitting a pinhead-sized target on Earth with a dart aimed randomly from space.

Falling into black holes is one matter; finding them is another. No single black holes have yet been discovered, for their bending effects on passing light beams are too small to show up. However, black holes which belong in binary systems can have a dramatic effect upon their companions, as they tear away huge gas streamers and heat them to X-ray emitting temperatures. At present, about half a dozen black holes in this category are believed to exist.

The life story of a star is one of a long losing battle against the force of gravity, but it does not live in vain. Ordinary stars such as the Sun continually lose matter, in stellar winds and later as planetary nebulae, which mixes up with the gas in space to form the next generation of stars. The coolest red giants grow surface layers of dust grains, destined to become the stuff of planets. But as far as we are concerned, the extravagant supergiant stars which explode as supernovae are the most important of all.

The last two supernovae in our Galaxy occurred in 1572 and 1604, and astronomers believe that we are well overdue for one at the moment. It is on the cards that such a spectacular star death will happen during our lifetimes.

When a supernova occurs, it flings into space all the chemical elements it once processed in its desperate bid to keep shining. Carbon, oxygen, nitrogen, neon, silicon, magnesium, iron and even heavier elements created in the holocaust itself drift and swirl among the gases destined to give birth to young stars and their planets. Among them are chemicals which are the seeds of life itself. We owe our existence in the ultimate resort not to water, nor to oxygen, nor to our happy location in the solar system, but to the fact that an exploding star impregnated our local gas cloud. How many more times has this happened in the history of the Universe?

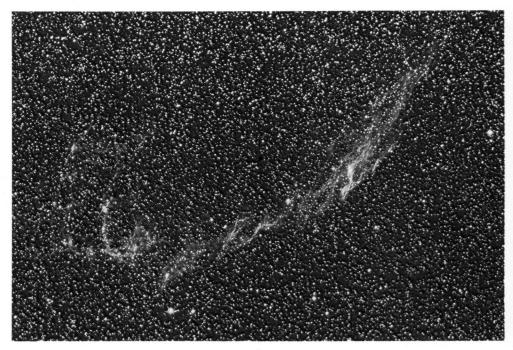

Starwrecks, ancient and modern.
above *The wisps of the Veil Nebula in Cygnus represent the remains of a star which exploded some 20,000 years ago. This arc of gas is just a portion of a huge circular shell called the Cygnus Loop, still slowly expanding into space and sweeping up matter before it. Ultimately the gas — enriched by material formed in the supernova explosion — will form into new generations of stars and planets.*

right *The Crab Nebula — 'the guts of a star spewed out into space' — is the result of a supernova which was seen to occur only 900 years ago. Chinese astronomers described the brilliant star which graced their night (and day) skies as looking like 'half a bamboo mat' when it exploded in AD 1054. The Crab is an exceedingly bright and atypical supernova remnant, whose energy derives from a rapidly spinning pulsar at its centre.*

IS THERE ANYBODY THERE?

No science fiction film or television series is nowadays complete without its fair complement of aliens. Whether bug-eyed monster or point-eared humanoid, friendly or destructive, extraterrestrial beings are undoubtedly real to the moviegoer and the television addict. They are the basis for phenomenally long-running television series such as the British *Dr Who* and the American *Star Trek*, and for box-office record breaking films, beginning with *2001: A Space Odyssey* and continuing through *Star Wars* and *Close Encounters of the Third Kind*, to *Alien* and *E.T.*

Is there any scientific basis for these imaginative, colourful and sometimes horrific creations — are there likely to be other intelligent beings in the Universe? At present Man has only two real facts to rely on: planet Earth supports life and there has been as yet no incontestable evidence for life elsewhere. In recent years, however, biologists and astronomers have together come much closer to understanding how life came to arise on the primitive Earth, and astronomers have concluded that Earth-like planets are likely to be 'two a penny' in our Galaxy. These advances make convincing grounds for believing that life could have evolved on other planets and that it is only the enormity of space which keeps us in ignorance of our cosmic family.

Life began on Earth very early in its history. Formed some 4,600 million years ago, its earliest fossils are all of 3,400 million years old. These are single-celled creatures preserved in the Fig Tree chert rocks of Swaziland. From such cells all life on Earth has evolved. All terrestrial life, from single-celled algae to Man, depends on the interactions of certain long organic molecules for their activities of growth, movement and reproduction: these are

right *A model of the DNA molecule. These twisted strands are located in the nucleus of every living cell and serve as a blueprint for the construction of the organism. They can also make copies of themselves. The evolution of such complex molecules is a prerequisite for life, one of the characteristics of which is the ability to reproduce, and the raw materials from which they are derived exist throughout the Universe.*

below *Dark 'holes' in this star field are dense clouds of obscuring dust grains in space. Inside these cool, undisturbed clouds, complex molecules, which may one day initiate life on a newborn planet, slowly build up from individual atoms.*

far right *A terrifying scene from Alien: slowly, inexorably, the creature starts to hatch out of its egg. Films like this remind us that alien life may not resemble terrestrial beings, nor may it share the same sense of values.*

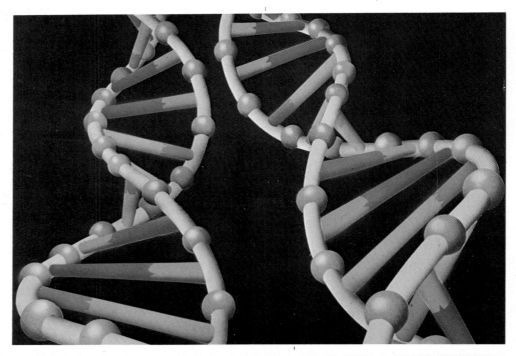

proteins and nucleic acids (DNA). The two essential types of organic molecule must have sprung into existence from the totally inanimate rocks and atmosphere of the early Earth.

At this time, around 4,000 million years ago, Earth was being pounded by in-falling meteorites which gouged out craters as large as any we see on the Moon; volcanoes were cloaking it with a lightning-racked atmosphere composed mainly of carbon dioxide, laced with noxious gases such as hydrogen sulphide, hydrogen cyanide and carbon monoxide; and from the unbroken cloud cover a continuous downpour of rain continued for millions of years. Yet these horrendous conditions were ideal for the genesis of life.

The atmospheric gases were disrupted by the meteorites' supersonic shock waves, the lightning bolts and ultraviolet light from the young Sun. They recombined into small organic molecules. The rain sluiced them into the seas, where they dissolved and reacted further to make up the basic ingredients of the proteins and nucleic acids. The Earth's warm, shallow oceans were at that time as rich in organic molecules as chicken soup!

Since the 1950s experiments on similar mixtures of gases in the laboratory have proved that Earth's oceans must have become a broth of suitable molecules. How these came together in cells, complete with the complex interlinked chemical reactions which are life's processes, is not at all certain at present. On the early Earth it somehow happened, and cells were

formed. From then on evolution to higher, multicelled life forms was only a matter of time. Plant cells absorbed virtually all the carbon dioxide from the atmosphere, replacing it with oxygen to give Earth its unusual atmosphere, unique in the solar system. Planets and animals invaded land. And eventually a self-styled intelligent species arose: Man.

For all his companionship of other animals and plants on Earth, Man is now consumed with the desire to discover whether the Universe contains other beings of similar — or superior — intellectual standing. Many astronomers have played the numbers game, trying to calculate the chances of intelligent life elsewhere, and, in particular, the number of planets bearing such creatures within our own Galaxy of 100,000 million stars.

The Sun is a very ordinary and commonplace type of star, and current theories of star formation, outlined in the last chapter, show that most stars will be born with an attendant family of planets. The planets nearest the star will naturally be small and rocky, rather than gas giants, and it is quite possible that an Earth-sized planet could lie at a suitable distance from the star for water to exist as a liquid. Its early history would then have exactly paralleled the Earth's, up to the stage of having oceans of primeval organic soup. From that point, perhaps life developed by whatever pathway it found on Earth.

Such was the optimistic thinking of the 1960s. If one star in a hundred has an Earth-like planet, life would have evolved on a

thousand million worlds in our Galaxy alone. Among these there must be many with living beings as intelligent as Man.

Peter van de Kamp of the Sproul Observatory, Pennsylvania, backed up the idea that planetary systems are common by his decades-long study of nearby stars. Carefully tracking their slow motion across the sky, he found that several do not move steadily in a straight line. Their paths are perturbed by the gravitational tug of unseen orbiting planets.

Although other astronomers have recently disputed Van de Kamp's results, no-one doubts that planetary systems are common. One planetary system surrounding the nearby star Vega, may even have been 'seen' by the IRAS satellite, which detected heat radiation from dust in the system.

The conditions required for life to form, and survive, may, however, be more critical than these early estimates suggested. The region around a star where a planet's surface is warmed to between 0 °C and 100 °C — at which liquid water can exist — is called the ecosphere. The Sun's ecosphere consists roughly of the space be-

The search for life on Mars. Two Viking lander craft touched down on the surface of the Red Planet in 1976 to sample the soil for primitive life-forms but the results — though difficult to interpret — seem to be negative. In the picture above, a lander surveys its rocky surroundings. Note the pink sky, a result of coloration by airborne dust. To the right, an artist's impression shows a Viking lander dropping away from an orbiter. Both of the 1976 orbiters went on to undertake a thorough photographic survey of the planet.

tween the orbits of Venus and Mars, and at first astronomers thought that the Earth would have blossomed wherever it lay in this belt. It now seems, however, that life would never have started if its distance from the Sun were even slightly different. The ecosphere is very narrow, and Earth is fortunately placed right in it.

Venus, although very like Earth at its birth, has been transformed into a barren, blistering hell, simply because it is marginally closer to the Sun. Venus's temperature never fell low enough for the steam from early volcanoes to condense to water, and the growing thick atmosphere raised its temperature higher still. Latest calculations reveal that Earth would have suffered the same fate as Venus if it had been only a little closer to the Sun.

Further out, Earth would have suffered the frozen fate of Mars. Although the search for life on Mars is by no means over, many scientists feel that Mars has always been too frigid to encourage life. Earth's temperature has dropped uncomfortably low during the great Ice Ages, and had it been but a little further from the Sun's warming fires, it too might have frozen solid. Without liquid water, life could never have begun.

The situation turns out to be worse for fainter, less massive stars. For many there is no habitable zone at all; and since these are the commonest stars in the Galaxy a large proportion of the niches where life was once thought to reside are eliminated.

The debate over life's first steps, the assembly of natural molecules into cells, is still provoking controversy. Neither astronomers nor biologists are yet decided whether this was a freak event, unlikely to happen in another planet's primeval soup oceans, or whether it is a natural consequence of the way carbon-based molecules prefer to react. In that case the designs for life are ultimately hidden in the basic laws of the Universe itself.

Astrophysicists Sir Fred Hoyle and Chandra Wickramasinghe have championed an extremely heretical view of life's origins. They take as their starting point recent observations by radio astronomers which show that small organic molecules occur in the gas and dust clouds of interstellar space. (One gas cloud near the centre of our Galaxy contains enough ethyl alcohol molecules to fill the Earth with proof liquor, were it hollow!) The radio astronomers' haul now stands at over 50 varieties of molecule. Hoyle and Wickramasinghe believe that these combine into living cells in the harsh conditions of space; that the obscuring dust clouds are not composed of sooty specks from giant stars but of 'freeze-dried' living cells; and that these cells settled on the primitive Earth to form the basis of life here. If their view, rejected by most scientists, is true, then life is extremely common and widespread in the Universe.

Even if planets of other stars have life — and estimates range from the optimists' thousand million or so life-bearing planets

to the dyed-in-the-wool pessimists' zero — there is no guarantee that it will have evolved into beings with high intelligence. Man has populated this planet for less than 0.1 per cent of its history and has been civilized for far less. An intelligent race may not wish to explore space, anyway, or to contact other beings across the Galaxy. On Earth only the ancient Greeks and the Western European culture stemming from the Greek-inspired Renaissance have had the urge to explore the physical world. The venerable and distinguished civilizations of the East never felt this compulsion until swayed by the West; their wisdom lay in other spheres.

If the Galaxy is peopled by other intelligent races, they may be sending messages to each other or to suspect stars in the hope of communicating with beings on planets circling them. Since 1960 a few radio astronomers around the world have taken time off from their regular observations and pointed their big dishes at nearby stars in the hope of receiving Man's first message from an alien culture. The first and most famous survey was Frank Drake's Project Ozma, named after the princess of the mythical land of Oz. Later projects have scanned over 600 stars, and none has yet met with any success.

Radio communication is certainly a good way to send interstellar messages. Radio waves pass unimpeded through dust clouds in space which block ordinary light, and a radio transmitter can send out a tremendously powerful beam. The world's largest radio telescope, a 305 metre (1000 foot)

diameter mesh bowl suspended in a hollow in the hills near Arecibo in Puerto Rico, could communicate with its like anywhere in our Galaxy—provided they were pointed towards each other. This highlights a major snag in interstellar eavesdropping. Unless someone out there is pointing his transmitter Sunwards at the same moment that our receiver is looking at his star, we will not get the message; and this coincidence is unlikely if he is transmitting to many stars in turn and we are 'listening in' to a programme of several hundred in rotation.

Another problem is choice of wavelength. A receiver must tune in to a specific wavelength, and it must obviously be the same wavelength as broadcast by our distant counterparts. We can only guess what that will be. Early searches, including Ozma, tuned in to 21 cm, the wavelength associated with the commonest element in the Universe — hydrogen. Since, there have been vast improvements in electronics. Microchip technology makes it possible to tune into many wavelengths simultaneously, and one new prototype receiver can cope with 74,000 bands at once.

Radio may not even be the obvious radiation to use for broadcasting, to a civilization millions of years more advanced than ours. Messages may be flying through interstellar space carried by light waves, infrared or ultraviolet radiation.

Whatever messenger is used, interstellar conversations must be long-winded affairs. No message can travel faster than Nature's

above *A space-age version of the message in a bottle. This plaque — Man's first attempt at communicating with extraterrestrial life — was attached to the planetary spaceprobes Pioneer 10 and 11, now heading out of the solar system into the realms of the stars. If these probes should ever be intercepted, their finders will be able to discover the location, and to some extent the nature, of the race that sent them. The lower part of the plaque shows the position of Earth in the solar system and the path of the probe; the radiating lines above map the position of the Sun relative to the nearest pulsars. The human figures provoked the most controversy: people objected to their nudity and the woman's passivity.*

left *Spaceship of the future? In addition to the conventional uses which have been suggested for the thousands of asteroids — such as mining them to exploit their mineral wealth — other, more outlandish proposals have been made. Some scientists believe that, hollowed-out and fitted with a propulsion system, asteroids would make ideal 'space-arks' for lengthy, multi-generation journeys to the stars.*

speed limit, the velocity of light, and so a message to even the nearest star would take over four years; almost nine years would elapse from our transmitted 'hello' to hearing their faint reply. Even the optimists calculate the nearest intelligent civilization to be around 100 light years away, so dialogue is out of the question. We would probably receive a comprehensive account of their planet, biology and culture without any need for prompting — each query would introduce an interruption in the message of a couple of centuries!

There is little point in all civilizations patiently listening in to other stars, if no one is transmitting any messages. We have, in fact, been unintentionally transmitting for the past 50 years: domestic radio and television signals leaking into space will have caught the attention of any listening-in civilizations within a 50 light year radius. If there is one some 25 light years away, a return message may be arriving right now.

We could listen in to others' domestic broadcasts if we had a large enough radio telescope. Optimists have prepared a detailed plan calling for an array of 1,000 radio telescopes, each as big as the largest present-day manoeuvrable radio telescopes. This patiently watching radio eye, named Cyclops, is unfortunately likely to remain firmly on the drawingboard, for there is little hope of any government being willing to fund it with the necessary billions of dollars.

Man has, in fact, sent an intentional message to the stars. In November 1974 scientists at the large Arecibo dish sent a message, in a dot—dash type of code, towards a large cluster of stars. Among the million or so stars covered by the telescope beam, there is a relatively high chance of one with a planet bearing a listening radio telescope. The message's immediate effect was to provoke an acrimonious debate on Earth: does a small group of scientists have

the right to proclaim our existence to the cosmos without consulting the Earth's population as a whole — or even their elected governments? Some scientists think it prudent not to advertise that planet Earth is hospitable, in case aliens prove to be as destructive — intentionally or accidentally — as some recent films have portrayed them. Since the star cluster is some 24,000 light years away, however, the outcome of this message will be a problem for our distant descendants.

Nearer home, spacecraft whose courses will carry them beyond the solar system have been used as interstellar visiting cards. Pioneers 10 and 11, which flew by and photographed Jupiter (and, for the latter, Saturn), bear an inscribed plaque showing the Sun's location relative to the nearest pulsars. This is a chart decipherable by any civilization which is technically advanced enough to capture the probe out in interstellar space. The Voyager 1 and 2 craft carry

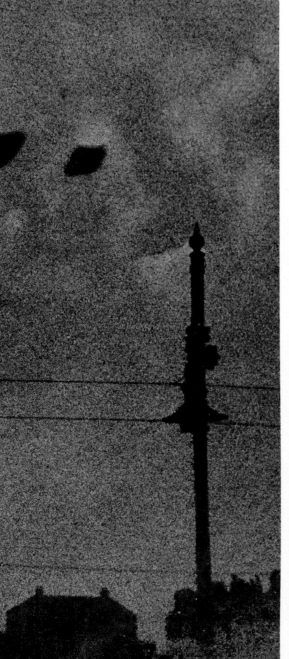

a sound record of events on Earth, including an audio sequence portraying the evolution of life on Earth.

These probes will reach the empire of the stars. Although they are not aimed at any particular star, their momentum will carry them to the distance of the nearest in some 80,000 years.

With present technology Man could even send an unmanned probe to the stars fast enough to arrive within a human lifetime. Detailed plans for this starship, named Daedalus, have been drawn up. Its fuel would be a rare type of helium, either made in Earth-orbiting nuclear reactors or scooped up from Jupiter's helium-rich atmosphere. The helium is fabricated into tiny nuclear bombs, which are exploded in a steady stream behind it to give Daedalus a continuous succession of pushes. It would reach its target, Barnard's star, in only 47 years. This star, the second-closest to the Sun after the Alpha Centauri triple system,

has two massive planets, according to Peter van de Kamp. The technology to create Daedalus exists today; all that is lacking is the will — and the money.

Gerard O'Neill, who devised the concept of space colonies to support millions of people in Earth orbit, foresees human exploration of the stars. One of his colonies, fitted with a nuclear reactor to provide light and heat in cold interstellar space and a suitable rocket drive, could take off from Earth orbit and cruise the stars. Slow and cumbersome it would be, and its passage from star to star would exceed a human lifetime, but these space arks could distribute the descendants of the original colonists throughout our Galaxy. Leaving settlements on all habitable planets they encounter, a fleet of space arks could colonize the entire Galaxy in a million years.

Long though this period may seem, it is short compared with the lifetime of the Galaxy and we are as yet only beginning to

'Close encounters of the third kind': three pictures of unidentified flying objects (UFOs), which are claimed by some to be spaceships from alien civilizations. The picture on the far left shows a UFO rising over a pine forest in Oregon, USA, taken in May 1964. In the middle picture, three UFOs fly in formation over Conisbrough, UK (photographed by Stephen Pratt on 28 March 1966). The photographer of the third UFO claims to have met the occupants of this craft, which appeared over America.

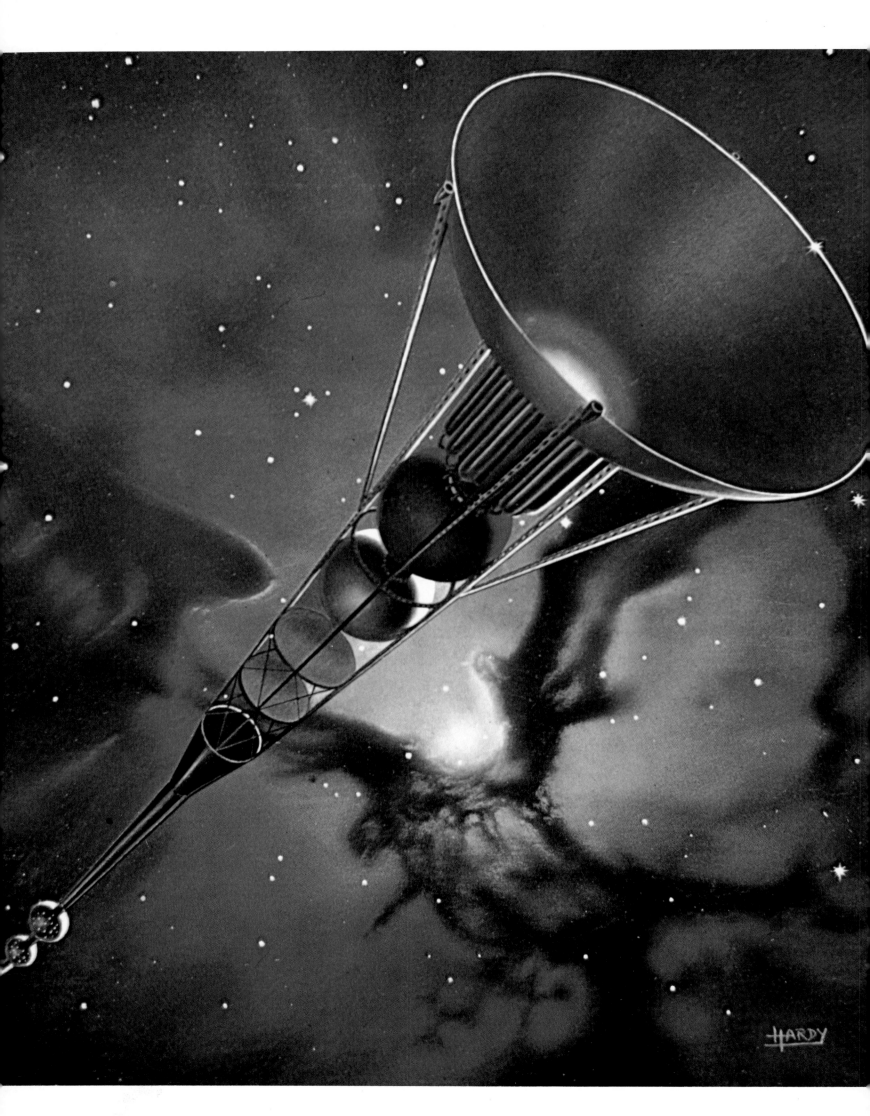

flex our space muscles. If space travel is this easy, however, why has Earth not been visited many times already by representatives of other civilizations which have flowered earlier?

We can dismiss claims made, supposedly in the name of science, of aliens appearing to ancient peoples of Earth and being taken for gods. Investigations of these claims — claims which have certainly sold their authors many books — have always revealed them to be distortions, exaggerations and sometimes downright lies.

The possibility that unidentified flying objects, UFOs, are alien spacecraft deserves more serious consideration. Although 90 per cent of UFO sightings prove to be misidentifications (of weather balloons, the planet Venus and other natural objects), there is a small core of unex-plained sightings. Professional astronomer Allen Hynek, who joined the United States Air Force investigation Project Blue Book as a sceptic, was eventually forced to accept that some sightings, made by separate reputable witnesses, cannot be explained on present-day knowledge. This does not mean they are alien spacecraft — 'flying saucers'. The few scientists such as Hynek who publicly admit that there may be something genuine in a small fraction of UFO sightings prefer to regard them as natural objects of some unknown kind. Most scientists, however, write off all UFO reports as misidentifications and believe that there is no case to present.

The Galaxy may, in fact, be teeming with alien life, but they — unlike some of Earth's nations — prefer to leave indigenous cultures alone. On this view, they have left us as a wildlife park in the outer reaches of the Galaxy, to observe how our primitive culture and technology progress.

The very absence of alien visitors suggests to present-day scientists that our civilization lies at one of two extremes. In the first view we are so primitive that Earth is regarded as a zoo; we are not advanced enough to join the 'Galactic Club', in veteran radio astronomer Ronald Bracewell's phrase. Alternatively, life is a very uncommon occurrence and we are the most advanced form of life, not only in our planetary system, but also in our entire Galaxy. In this case our space journeys so far have not really taken us even as far as our front door. Man has a whole Galaxy to explore and make his own — and then, perhaps, he will move on to the rest of the galaxies in the Universe.

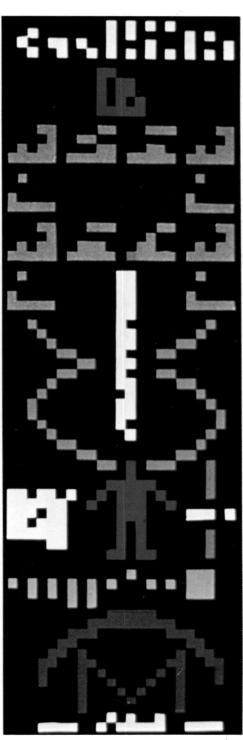

left A photon rocket glides swiftly across the face of the Trifid Nebula, bound for some remote part of our Galaxy. Although this scene belongs in the very far future, it is only by developing rockets like this that we will get to the stars. The present generation of chemically fuelled rockets is too heavy and too slow; but this rocket is propelled into space by a beam of light, and so can reach speeds approaching the velocity of light itself. A team of scientists belonging to the British Interplanetary Society already have plans for a starship on the drawing-board. 'Daedalus' is unlikely ever to be built, but the study has shown that travel to the stars — in a craft powered by the explosion of small hydrogen bombs, and capable of reaching speeds one-tenth the speed of light — is not forever impossible.

above and right Lying in a natural hollow in the mountains of Puerto Rico, the Arecibo 305 metre (1000 ft) fixed radio dish is the biggest in the world. Normally it is used in a receiving mode to pick up radiowaves from objects in space, but in November 1974, it broadcast a coded message (right) towards a dense cluster of 300,000 stars. On/off pulses of the signal, when properly arranged, make up the grid pattern. This shows a representation of the numbers 1 to 10 (top row), and the atomic numbers of the elements which make up life (beneath). The winding strands depict the DNA molecule, beneath which stands a human figure atop a representation of the solar system. The final section shows the Arecibo telescope itself. It will take 24,000 years for this declaration of our existence to arrive at its destination.

BEGINNINGS AND ENDINGS

Despite its 100,000 million stars, our vast Galaxy is but a speck in space. Yet well into this century, astronomers believed it to be the whole Universe, and, standing outside under the inky dome of an early autumn night, it is easy to see why. Thousands of diamond-hard points of light are strewn limitlessly across the velvet backdrop. In a pair of binoculars the misty overhead arch of the Milky Way is revealed as a seemingly infinite number of stars and starclouds, all of them packed together so tightly as to be beyond belief.

However, this crowding is just a perspective effect, arising from the Sun's position inside the disc of our flattened Milky Way Galaxy. Looking along the disc, more remote stars appear concentrated together in a band; above and below the disc, stars thin out. The presence of the Milky Way in our skies is proof positive that we belong to a Galaxy of stars.

Making sense of our Galaxy's structure is complicated by the fact that we live inside it: a real case of not being able to see the wood for the trees. But although we cannot — as

yet — hover outside, there are plenty of other galaxies to compare ours with, and astronomers think that they now have a pretty good idea of the Milky Way's geography. From the side it looks (in the words of one astronomer) 'like two fried eggs clapped together back to back', with the Sun and its family well in the 'white', some two-thirds of the way out. Seen from above, it takes on a more dignified appearance: a vast spiral catherine-wheel of stars, gas and dust, spinning slowly in space. Here we can drop our accustomed modesty, for it is a giant among galaxies, measuring some 100,000 light years across.

Our position in the Galaxy's disc affords us grandstand views of starbirth, with all its attendant beauties: gas and dust clouds, glowing nebulae and clustered young stars. Starbirth is at its busiest in the spiral arms which thread the disc, for these are zones of compression — 'density waves' set up by a combination of our Galaxy's rotation and its gravity — where the abundant disc gas is squeezed into action. Taking 250 million years to make a circuit of the Galaxy, our

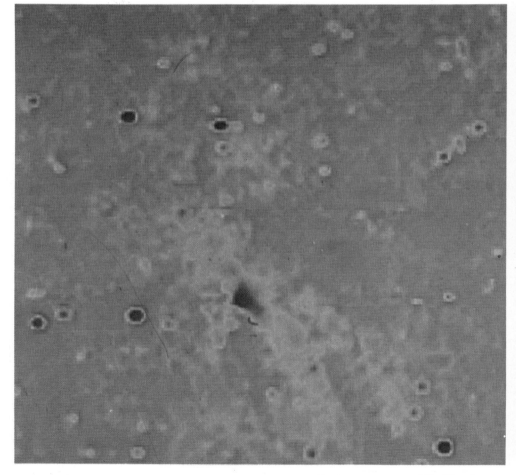

above *Penetrating the haze of dust which dogs the optical astronomer, this photograph taken in long-wavelength infrared radiation reveals previously-hidden regions near the heart of our own Milky Way Galaxy.*

right *Half as large again as our Milky Way, the great Andromeda galaxy appears very much as ours must when seen from outside. The streak is the track of a satellite which crossed the field when the picture was being taken.*

Sun passes through many gas-rich spiral arms along the way, leading some astronomers to speculate that these passages may trigger Ice Ages on Earth or the formation of new comets.

Moving towards the centre of our Galaxy, 30,000 light years away, we might expect our skies to become more vivid still: and yet the reverse happens. Once the nuclear bulge — the 'yolk' — of our Galaxy is reached, the variety we are accustomed to has gone, replaced by an unchanging vista of old, red stars. The nucleus of our Galaxy contains no dust, no gas; starbirth ceased long ago. Only at the uttermost core of our Galaxy are circumstances any different. Astronomers picking up radio waves and infrared radiation from this innermost sanctum — invisible to our eyes, being dimmed a hundred thousand million times by the dust which chokes our Galaxy's disc — tell of bizarre conditions there. Stars are packed together 300 million times more closely than normal, making nearest neighbours a mere 4 light *days* apart. Supersized

young stars are believed to be forming, and massive gas clouds are being flung out from the centre, speeding away from a powerful radio source which marks the position of our Galaxy's heart.

Our Galaxy is fuzzily bounded by a spheroidal 'halo' of ancient stars, a relic of the distant days when the Milky Way was a gas cloud. Many of these stars swarm together in globular clusters, balls of more than a hundred thousand stars, while others roam the emptiness. But how empty is the halo? New evidence suggests that our halo — and those of other galaxies — may be far more massive than the visible disc. The form of the dark 'hidden' mass is still unknown.

Beyond the halo is empty space. Save for a few stars and globulars which may have leaked away from our Galaxy's pull, there is nothing — no gas, no stars and no planets. That is, until we reach the next galaxy.

Even the closest galaxies are 160,000 light years away, and from there they stretch to the limits of present-day telescopes — a

distance of some 10,000 million light years. They come in almost all shapes and sizes. About half of those we see are spiral galaxies like our own, and one, the great Andromeda galaxy, is, at 2¼ million light years, the most remote object visible to the unaided eye. In the past, astronomers classified spiral galaxies according to their subtleties of appearance, and secret lists of 'favourites' testify to their individual characters. But in common with one another all spirals have ancient haloes, old nuclear bulges and clumpy arms studded with shining gas clouds strung out like pearls.

Like the spirals, irregular galaxies, which make up only a small proportion of the total, are rich in gas and young stars. They are small galaxies; too small, it seems, to 'grow' spiral arms. Two of the most famous are the southern hemisphere's Magellanic Clouds, discovered by Ferdinand Magellan on his round-the-world voyage in 1521. Looking like detached portions of the Milky Way, these are actually galaxies in their own right, although less than a quarter the size of

our own. As far as we know, these are our closest extragalactic neighbours. Even if not true 'satellites' of the Milky Way, they make their presence felt by virtue of a huge bridge of cold hydrogen gas which links them to us and still awaits a convincing explanation.

Elliptical galaxies, the other main kind, are strangely lacking in character compared with their spiral and irregular cousins. They all look rather like spiral galaxies bereft of their arms: just swarms of old, red stars ranging in shape from round footballs, through flattened rugby balls to elongated spindles. To compensate, they have the greatest range in size of all the galaxies. At one end, the dwarf ellipticals are the most diminutive and probably the commonest galaxies in the Universe, each only one-hundredth of the size of ours. Their faintness prevents us from seeing all but the very nearest — those which belong to our small 'Local Group' of galaxies — and their extreme sparseness would surely disappoint a resident astronomer, who would only ever see three or so stars in his sky!

At the other extreme, giant elliptical galaxies of more than a million million stars are the biggest objects in the Universe. Most inhabit the centres of dense clusters of thousands of galaxies, and may have grown to their present sizes by 'feeding' on nearby neighbours.

Whether spiral, elliptical or irregular, all these galaxies would be considered 'normal' by an astronomer. But there are exceptions. One or two out of every hundred galaxies has suffered, or is suffering, disruption on such a scale that its entire character has altered. 'Exploding galaxies' are a phenomenon of the past 20 years' research, and astronomers believe that they may hold the key to understanding how galaxies are born.

At first sight, Seyfert galaxies (named after Carl Seyfert, who identified them) look like nearby spirals with exceptionally faint arms. But this is a contrast effect: their light is overwhelmingly dominated by the brilliance of their nuclear regions, where huge clouds of hot gas are hurled into the

outer parts of the galaxy at speeds of up to 7,000 km per second (almost 16 million miles per hour!). The culprit, astronomers believe, lurks right at the core; a tiny, intensely brilliant point of light no more than a few light months across. And yet this region, which is comparable in size with our own solar system, contains as much energy as our entire Galaxy consisting of 100,000 million stars.

Astronomers had but a brief time to boggle at this before finding that they had uncovered only the tip of the iceberg — galaxies exist which are more violent still. There came reports of radio galaxies: remote supergiant ellipticals giving out as much energy in radio waves as they did in light. Although the light came from the galaxy itself, the radio waves originated in two huge clouds of charged particles, one on either side of its main body, which had clearly started life in the galaxy's disturbed core. Once again, astronomers hit the energy problem head on, for the clouds were often separated by millions of light

above Looking like a detached portion of the Milky Way in the skies of the southern hemisphere, the Large Magellanic Cloud is the closest galaxy to our own. Although only one quarter the Milky Way's size, this irregular galaxy is made up of over a thousand million stars and is studded with bright gas clouds (like the Tarantula Nebula, towards the right) where stars are still forming.

left The spiral galaxy known as NGC 1097 spins serenely in the depths of space, attended by its small elliptical companion (lower right). The colours in this photograph are false, and are designed to highlight regions in the galaxy which are of special interest to astronomers.

overleaf From very near to very far: this picture shows the remote quasar 3C 273 (right) captured by the X-ray cameras aboard the orbiting Einstein Observatory. At top left is a new find: a quasar lying at the staggering distance of 10,000 million light years, which has just been detected as an X-ray emitter. X-rays can be produced only by objects which are either excessively hot or highly energetic; quasars appear to be both. Speckles here arise from 'noise' in the detector.

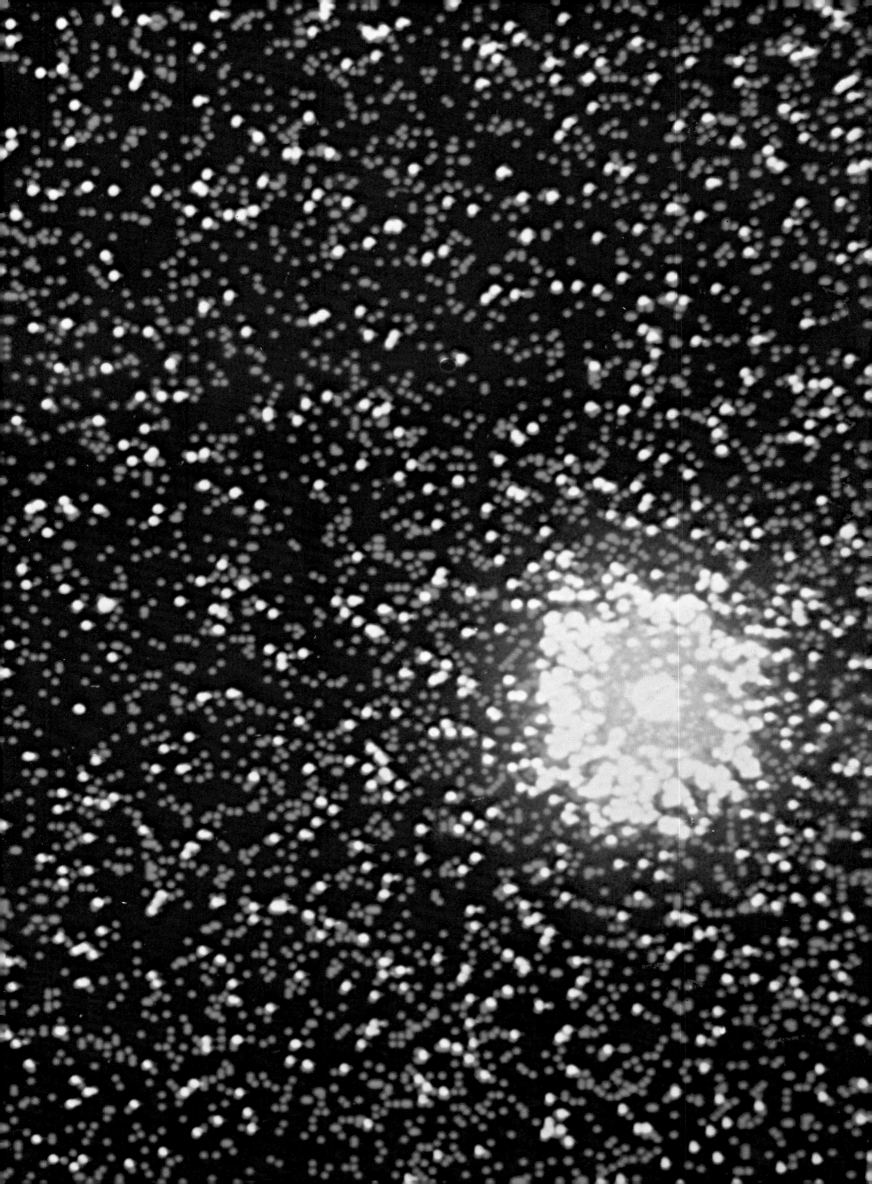

years and had been sent on their way at speeds approaching one-tenth of the velocity of light. As if once were not enough, some radio galaxies showed evidence for several core explosions.

None of this had prepared astronomers for quasars. First discovered in 1963, they looked like nearby stars — hence the name quasi-stellar objects, to give them their full title — but at 10,000 million light years they turned out to be far more distant than even the remotest galaxies. But galaxies they are; or, more accurately, the brilliant cores of active galaxies. Quasars are the most luminous and energetic objects in the Universe, packing the equivalent of a million million stars into a core only light months across to fuel their cataclysmic eruptions.

Yet there is a pattern to all this wanton destruction, and to discern it we must look to the message of light. Because light takes time to reach us from bodies in space, we always see them as they were in the past — at the time when the light was emitted. For nearby objects the delay is not serious: we see the Sun as it was 8⅓ minutes ago, the nearest star 4⅓ years in the past. And the same goes for close galaxies — the 2¼ million year gulf between the Andromeda galaxy and our own is hardly an instant in

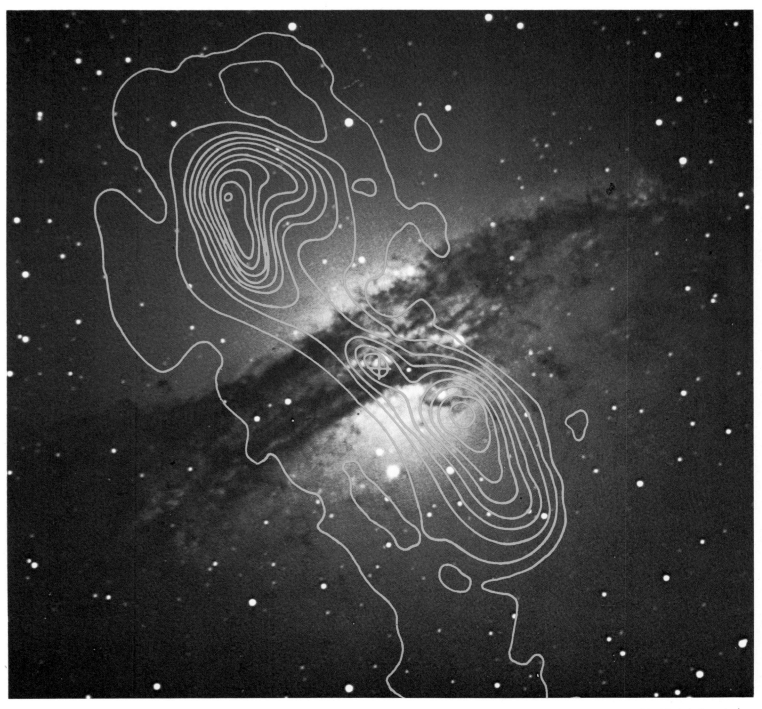

left *Seated beneath the 2.5 metre (98 inch) mirror of the UK's Isaac Newton Telescope, an astronomer takes detailed photographs of spectra using the Image Tube Spectrograph. Without large telescopes and sensitive light-analysing equipment, our knowledge of distant galaxies and the still-more remote quasars would be very meagre.*

above *A key to the quasar mystery? A powerful explosion has disrupted the heart of the supergiant elliptical galaxy Centaurus A, resulting in the ejection of two plasma clouds which show up only at radio wavelengths (the superimposed contour maps were made with a radiotelescope). Radio galaxies like this may represent a later stage in the life of a quasar.*

overleaf *A supermassive black hole lurks at the heart of an active galaxy, greedily swallowing stars and gas unwary enough to come too close. Most of the infalling matter forms into a dizzily-whirling 'accretion disc' surrounding the hole, which glares dazzlingly as matter spirals in with speeds close to the velocity of light. Astronomers believe that the strange conditions in and around this accretion disc can help to explain how active galaxies and quasars work.*

their lives. But we see the quasars as they were 10,000 million years ago, only a short time after the Universe began. To put it another way, quasars are at an extremely young stage.

Using this technique of backwards crystal-gazing, astronomers think they can work out how galaxies came into being. The early Universe, they believe, was filled with turbulent gas clouds. Under its own gravity, each cloud started to contract, making stars first in its outer regions, and then ever more quickly towards the increasingly dense centre. If the proto-galaxy was big enough, the core density would continue to rise unchecked until the matter ultimately coalesced into a supersized black hole.

The massive black hole is the power-house of a violent young galaxy. Messily swallowing stars and gas which come its way from the galaxy's continued collapse, it becomes surrounded by a swirling vortex of gas and debris, which is given vast amounts of energy by the black hole's gravitational field. Astronomers believe that the light of quasars may come from this glaring accretion disc.

The accretion disc does not merely glare; it is capable of many acts of violence, such as the ejection of gas clouds and charged particles into space far beyond the galaxy. A former quasar would look like a radio galaxy, at present quiet, but surrounded by evidence of its troubled youth. These slightly older galaxies have finished collapsing, and so their black hole's fuel supply has dried up — but should sufficient gas chance on the core region, another eruption can be powered. Even so, radio galaxies bring on their own extinction by driving out the gas which helps both to generate their power and to make new stars. There must be many dead radio galaxies among the giant ellipticals near us today.

Spiral galaxies, never as big as their elliptical brothers, have a less chequered history. With proportionally smaller black holes at their hearts, their youth was less violent, and the young galaxies were never totally scoured of the gas earmarked for future starbirth. But nearby Seyfert galaxies remind us that we should never be complacent: violence can still take place in ordinary spirals should there be sufficient gas in the core, and there are some astronomers who even consider that our own Milky Way could well be a potential hazard in this respect.

For all the tangled intricacies of their lives, galaxies are merely flotsam bobbing on the vast ocean of the Universe, and its swell is carrying them inexorably apart. We see this expansion of the Universe as a recession of all the galaxies — or the clusters of galaxies, to be exact — from our own. But we are in no way being avoided, for the picture would look the same from any galaxy in the Universe.

By backtracking the motions of all the galaxies, astronomers arrive at a time some 15,000 million years in the past when they were all together. Space and time were both set to zero. And then the greatest act of violence in the history of the Universe was perpetrated: its very own birth by means of the 'Big Bang'.

Particle physicists and cosmologists (astronomers who study the structure and evolution of the Universe as a whole) have worked closely together to discover what happened in the Big Bang. Amazingly, they find that the content of our Universe was determined in the first 200 seconds of its existence: all the atomic particles we know today were created in an intense blaze of gravity and radiation, during which time other particles were allowed to live briefly before being weeded out. A very slight change in the initial conditions of temper-

The trace below is the spectral signature of the remote quasar OH471, recorded in unprecedented detail by Alec Boksenberg and his colleagues. The spikes on the trace are the spectral lines produced by different elements in the quasar; detailed measurement of these can reveal a lot about the conditions inside the source. Professor Alec Boksenberg (far left) is seen adjusting the revolutionary detector he designed to obtain spectra from extremely faint objects such as this. Called the IPCS (Image Photon Counting System), Boksenberg's ultra-fast device catches individual photons (bundles of light) from distant objects, which it then amplifies millions of times before they are recorded. A photograph of the quasar (arrowed) is shown at left; even in the world's biggest telescopes it is scarcely visible. Hundreds of even fainter, more remote quasars should be picked up by the Space Telescope in the late 1980s.

Radio telescopes at Cambridge (right) turned up some of the first evidence to suggest that the never-changing 'Steady State' picture of the Universe was not the correct one. By discovering that the number of radiosources which existed in the early Universe was greater than it is today, the radioastronomers demonstrated that the Universe does change with time. Another radiotelescope (below) — this time a former satellite-tracking antenna in New Jersey, USA — finally laid the Steady State theory to rest for once and for all by detecting the 3K Background Radiation. Most astronomers believe that this represents the cooled-down relic of a very hot 'Big Bang' in which the Universe began. Today, we see the effect of this traumatic birth in the expansion of the Universe: all the clusters of galaxies (like the Hercules Cluster, below right) are moving away from each other with speeds proportional to their distances. In the light of present evidence, it appears that there is not enough matter in the Universe to halt this relentless flight: it will continue to expand forever.

ature, pressure or rate of expansion would have created an entirely different Universe.

Although the Big Bang theory has been championed by many astronomers over the past few decades, there have always been those, both astronomers and laymen, who have found the concept of an instantaneous creation emotionally and philosophically unsatisfying. But a chance discovery made in the mid-1960s, now confirmed beyond dispute, seems to prove that the Big Bang really did happen.

In 1965 American radio astronomers Arno Penzias and Robert Wilson 'borrowed' a satellite-tracking antenna from the Bell Telephone Laboratories to look for very faint radio signals from the outskirts of our Galaxy. The horn-shaped antenna was one of the most sensitive in the world, but try as they might, the astronomers could not eradicate a constant background noise in the receiver. At one point they had to get rid of a pair of pigeons, their attendant droppings and an egg — 'by decisive means' — but still the noise did not clear up. After consultations with colleagues at nearby Princeton University, they were forced to the conclusion that the noise was not in their telescope: it was radiation coming evenly from the whole sky.

The temperature of the radiation was only 2.7 °C above the absolute zero of temperature (−273 °C), but it had to be coming from somewhere — and its smoothness (isotropy) meant somewhere ex-

tremely far away. Princeton theorists Robert Dicke and Jim Peebles tracked down its source to the Big Bang itself. Their calculations showed that the '3 K Background Radiation' had arisen at a time a little after the Big Bang when the Universe was very hot, but as the Universe expanded, the glare had cooled until it was finally a barely detectable ember.

The discovery sounded the death-knell for Fred Hoyle's then-popular 'Steady State' theory (which said that the Universe had always been, and always will be, the same) and set people wondering what the Universe held in store for them in the future. Astronomers started to ask: 'Will the Universe expand for ever? Or will it collapse and be reborn in another Big Bang?'

The present evidence marginally supports the first of these alternatives. Astronomers can look at galaxies as they were in the distant past and at galaxies as they are now in the almost-present; and then they can compare the Universe's expansion rate at these two times. It shows no signs of slowing down, as we would expect if the Universe were destined to collapse again. And collapse, if it is ever to occur, will be masterminded by the force of gravity — by the pull of all the galaxies and clusters of galaxies in the Universe upon one another. Even making generous allowances for 'missing mass' (invisible dark matter in space), we still need at least ten times more matter than we can see to brake the

expansion of the Universe. In the long run, it seems gravity loses.

And so, unless the sensitive Space Telescope tells us otherwise, our future belongs to a forever-expanding Universe. There will be no 'Big Crunch' to be dreaded one day. The galaxies will continue to fly apart, making stars and planets until their gas reserves are gone. As the last stars die, life may find it hard to make headway, although by then, in the inconceivably remote future, living beings will probably have found a multitude of ways to harness other forms of energy for their needs — and this includes tapping the formidable power of a spinning black hole.

If Man were to make space his destiny, then this future could be his heritage: not just one overcrowded planet, but a whole galaxy of 100,000 million stars. Should he develop ways of travelling close to the speed of light, the laws of relativity will ensure that he could cover a substantial fraction of the Universe in his lifetime. But if he sees his future permanently tied to Earth, he has signed his own death warrant — dwindling resources, overcrowding and war will take care of that. And in the event that we are the only living beings in our Milky Way, do we not have a responsibility to stay alive?

Astronomers have done their best to chart the seas, test the wind and generally prepare the way ahead. For our future's sake, let us not ignore the challenge.

INDEX

Page numbers in bold type refer to illustrations or their captions

Acknowledgements

The publishers would like to thank the following individuals and organisations for their kind permission to reproduce the photographs in this book:

Photograph by P.J. Andrews/D.A. Calvert Royal Greenwich Observatory 16; Ron Arbour 18 left; Arecibo Observatory, NAIC, Cornell University 81 left and right; Aspect Picture Library Title Page, 6-7 below, 8-9, 33, 40 left, 48, 50-51, 52 below, 62-63, 68 above; Association of Universities for Research in Astronomy, Inc., The Kitt Peak National Observatory (Science Photo Library) Half Title, 60, 61 above, (Science Photo Library) 82-83, (Science Photo Library) 89; Derek Bayes/Aspect 24-25; Courtesy of Bell Laboratories 94 below; Professor Alex Boksenberg, University College, London 92 above, 92-93 below, 93 above; California Institute of Technology and Carnegie Institute of Washington (1961) 66-67, 68 below; Institute of Astronomy, University of Cambridge 54 below; J. Allan Cash Ltd. 94 above; Celestron International 61 below; Colorific (Earl Young) 40-41; Dr. R.J. Dufour 89 (overlay); Mary Evans Picture Library 14 above, 15 left and right; Fabbri Editori 72 above; Fortean Picture Library (Dr. Daniel Fry) 78 left, (Stephen Pratt) 78-79, (Dr. Daniel Fry) 79 right; Harry Ford, Mills Observatory, Dundee 17 below; Susan Griggs Agency Ltd. 12-13; Martin Grossmann 55; The Hale Observatories, California Institute of Technology 6 above right, 17 above, (Science Photo Library) 69, (1959 California Institute of Technology and Carnegie Institute of Washington) 70 left, 70-71, (Science Photo Library) 82 left, 95; David A. Hardy (Fantasy and Science Fiction, May 1979) 76, (The New Challenge of the Stars, Mitchell Beazley, 1977) 80; Dr. Carl Heiles (Science Photo Library) 24 inset; The Image Bank (Harold Sund) Endpapers, 7 above left; Gary Ladd, 1972 18-19; John Lorre (Science Photo Library) 84; Michael J. De Faubert Maunder 46 left, 46-47; Kenneth J. Medway 27; University of Michigan (Professor Miller) 58-59; NASA 7 above right, (Science Photo Library) 8 left, 10, 11 above and below, 28-29, 30-31, 32, 34, 36 above and below, 37, 42, (Science Photo Library) 44-45, 49 above and below, 52 above, 53, 74, 75, 77, 86-87; The National Maritime Museum, London 14 below; Novosti Press Agency 20-21, 35; Photri 43; Popperfoto 28 left; Royal Greenwich Observatory 88; The Royal Observatory, Edinburgh, 1978 21 right, 64 below, 65, 85; Dr. Richard Scaddan 22 below, 23; Courtesy of the Smithsonian Astrophysical Observatory 22 above; Gordon Solberg/Rimfire Photography 56 left; Twentieth Century-Fox Film Company Ltd. 73; U.S. Geological Survey 54 above, 64 above; U.S. Naval Observatory (Science Photo Library) 72 below; Harry Vine, Imperial College, London 56-57; John Walsh/Aspect Contents

Photograph from "Alien" courtesy of Twentieth Century-Fox Film Company Ltd.